TAT TVAM ASI

तत् त्वम् असि

YOU ARE THAT...
A Journey from Limitation to Possibilities

Dr. Anamika Bajpai, PhD, MBA

FanatiXx® Publication

FanatiXx® Publication
Rourkela | Mumbai | Delhi NCR | Ahmedabad

Tat Tvam Asi
By Dr. Anamika Bajpai, PhD, MBA

ISBN: 978-93-7406-170-1 (Paperback)

ISBN: 978-93-7406-187-9 (E-Book)

First Edition – 2026

For permissions, inquiries, or feedback:
Email: outreach@fanatixx.info
Instagram: @fanatixxpublication

Acknowledgement

No journey of becoming is solitary. While this book carries my reflections, it has been shaped by the guidance, discipline, and generosity of many individuals and institutions across different phases of my life. I remain sincerely grateful to everyone who influenced my journey — directly or indirectly.

My early years at **Saraswati Shishu Mandir** grounded me in structure and values. My time at **A.N.D. Mahila Mahavidyalaya, Kanpur**, further strengthened my academic foundation and self-belief. At **Bundelkhand University**, the study of forensic science redirected my path toward research. Securing admission to the M.Sc. program, followed by qualifying the UGC-JRF, became defining turning points that reshaped my confidence and trajectory.

I am deeply grateful to **Dr. Harsh Sharma**, whose seriousness toward scholarship shaped my early professional outlook, and to **Dr. Asha Srivastava**, my first role model in scientific and administrative leadership. Observing her expanded my understanding of disciplined and dignified authority.

My PhD advisor **Dr. K. N. Prasad** and mentors during doctoral training at **SGPGIMS, Lucknow** strengthened my commitment to research integrity and intellectual accountability.

In the United States, my growth continued through research and academic engagements at **Temple University** and later at **Drexel University**. I remain particularly thankful to **Dr. Kara Spiller**, my first postdoctoral mentor, from whom I learned clarity in communication, thoughtful presentation, and the courage to pursue excellence while accepting imperfection.

I am grateful to **Dr. Sheela Mishra**, Dean of Science, University of Lucknow, for her warmth, thoughtful conversations, and quiet encouragement. Her spiritual depth and dignified leadership have been a reassuring presence in my journey.

Across India and the United States, colleagues, collaborators, students, and friends have shaped me in ways both visible and subtle. I recognize myself as a small expression within a larger divine rhythm — formed by time, circumstance, and the people around me. Whatever clarity these pages carry is not mine alone.

To the reader: if these reflections encourage thoughtful perseverance and independent inquiry, this work has fulfilled its purpose.

Dedication

This book is dedicated to my ancestors,
whose invisible sacrifices made my visible journey possible.

To my Nana and Nani,
whose home was the soil where my earliest roots found strength.

To my parents and siblings,
who gave me roots strong enough to stand,
and love and trust deep enough to step beyond what they had known.

To my husband, Srikanth,
whose quiet strength, progressive spirit, and unwavering partnership gave me the freedom to continue becoming — never limiting my path, only standing beside me as I walked it.

And to my daughter,
so that she may always know that her path belongs to her.
And Almighty lights her path.....

Foreword

Education is not only a pathway to professional advancement; it is a formative process through which individuals learn to think clearly, navigate uncertainty, and develop a sense of purpose. For students - particularly those progressing through academic pathways without consistent guidance or exposure; this journey involves difficult decisions made quietly and often in isolation.

Tat Tvam Asi (You are that...) offers a reflective narrative that brings attention to these less visible dimensions of learning and growth. Through lived academic and professional experience, the author traces a journey shaped not by early certainty or privilege, but by sustained effort, discipline, and adaptability.

Rather focusing solely on outcomes, the book emphasizes process of: (a). how choices are made in the absence of mentorship, (b). how transitions across disciplines and institutions are managed, and (c). how resilience and confidence gradually take shape through responsibility, persistence, and experience. In doing so, the narrative reflects the realities encountered by many students within India's diverse educational landscape.

Drawing gently from India's philosophical tradition while remaining grounded in real educational and professional contexts, the work avoids prescription or ideology. Instead, it invites reflection, long-term thinking, and respect for learning as a lifelong discipline.

At a time, when rapid results are often emphasized, this book offers a covert perspective: that meaningful academic, professional, and societal contributions emerge through ethical effort, patience, and clarity of intent. It is my hope that this work will resonate with students, educators, and readers who value education as a foundation for thoughtful and responsible engagement with the world rather merely as a means to an end.

Prof. (Dr.) Asha Srivastava
Dean, School of Behavioral Forensics
National Forensic Sciences University
[An Institution of National Importance]
Ministry of Home Affairs, Government of India
Sector-9,Gandhinagar Gujarat 382007

गृह मंत्रालय
MINISTRY OF
HOME AFFAIRS
सत्यमेव जयते

Epigraph

तत्त्वमसि, You are that.

Author's Note

This book was not written because my journey was extraordinary. It was written because, for a long time, I believed my life was average and ordinary—and therefore limited.

I come from a background where ambition had to be practical, where responsibilities arrived early, and where options were not always visible. Like many students from modest families and small towns, I learned to adapt before I learned to dream. For years, I did not even recognize this pattern as being "stuck." It simply felt like life.

This book is for those who grew up without access to exposure, guidance, or a wide vocabulary of possibilities. For those who are capable but cautious. For those who are hardworking yet unsure. For those who carry family expectations, financial constraints, or inherited fears so quietly that they forget to ask what they themselves want.

My story moves through education, science, immigration, marriage, motherhood, pauses, and reinvention. But this is not a book about achievements. It is a book about becoming,, slowly, imperfectly, and often without a clear roadmap.

Pausing is human. Stopping is a choice we make only when we lose faith in ourselves. If this book offers you anything, I hope it is permission, to question the limits you inherited, to explore paths in uncertainty, and to trust that becoming is an extension of where you come from, not a rejection of it.

Letter to the Reader

Dear Students,

I'm writing to you because the word "average" has been used far too often to make people feel small.

Maybe you grew up in a place where no one talked about options. Maybe you did what was expected of you, not what excited you. Maybe you've failed quietly, doubted yourself deeply, or wondered why confidence comes so easily to others.

Feeling contained does not mean you are incapable. Often, it simply means you were never shown how wide the world can be.

You don't have to be exceptional to matter. You don't have to be fearless to move forward. You don't have to know your destination to take the next step.

Pause when life asks you to., But don't disengage from your curiosity. Don't label yourself so narrowly that you forget how adaptable you are.

You are allowed to grow slowly. You are allowed to change direction. You are allowed to become more than you imagined.

With faith in your becoming,
Anamika

Family & Context

(Where I Come From)

I am from very conservative middle class family background in Bharat.

I did not grow up in one home. I was raised in two.
I was born into my parents' family at Kanpur, Uttar Pradesh, but my early years were shaped almost entirely by my maternal grandparents at Unnao with my Nana-Shri Prakash Narayan Mishra and Nani-SMT. Sunder Devi Mishra. I used to call them Mummy-Papa. Until the age of thirteen, I lived with them. That home was my first universe. It was where I learned everything, faith before fear, curiosity before caution, and love without conditions.

My Nana was my emotional anchor and my first teacher. He spoke to me as if my questions mattered. He listened with patience and trust. My Nani wrapped daily life in warmth, through food, rituals, stories, and quiet reassurance. Their home felt expansive, not because of space, but because of emotional freedom. God felt close there. Childhood felt unhurried.

At the age of thirteen, I moved to Kanpur to live with my parents.
It felt less like a transition and more like a **lateral entry into a life already in motion**.

My parents had built their home in Kanpur within the framework of a traditional, conservative brahmin middle-class North Indian family. My father, Shri Shyam Kishor Bajpai, runs a small machinery-parts business. My mother, Smt. Madhubala Bajpai, is a full-time homemaker. Ours is a deeply religious home. Faith is not symbolic but lived. Rituals are woven into daily life. God is part of routine, not reserved for crisis.

At the time I joined them, our family consisted of my parents, my younger sister Niharika, and me. In the years that followed, our family grew. Another sister, Vidhi, was born in 2000, and my brother, Modak in 2004. With each child, love multiplied, but so did responsibility. We lived in a modest two-bedroom rented place. Space was shared. Time was managed carefully.

Silence was rare. Academic studies often happened in stolen moments from young kids- early mornings, late nights, and pauses between household rhythms. In Kanpur, I did not grow up surrounded by a strong academic environment. There were no doctors, engineers, or lawyers in my circle whose journeys I could observe. There were hardly any science students in my residential area. I had no direct exposure to career paths due to the protective structure and boundaries within which I was raised. Most girls studied until marriage, and boys until they found a way to earn a living. My father came from a worldview shaped not by exposure, but by responsibility. Families like ours did not travel widely or imagine many alternatives. Safety was love. Structure was care. Reputation mattered, especially where daughters were concerned. My parents and grandparents

gave me very strong value system, and taught me great sense of humility, courage and resilience.
In many families of that time, girls were naturally viewed as responsibilities to be carefully guided until a certain age. Sons were often given more visible freedom. This was not unusual; it was the social norm. My parents were not extreme in this regard. They were only deeply protective, shaped by their time, surroundings, and the quiet pressures of society.

For me, however, this environment felt very different from the world I had known with my Nana and Nani.
I had already lived a childhood where questions were encouraged, and independence grew gently. So, when I began to dream beyond familiar boundaries, to travel for education and imagine a life not fully mapped yet, I was, without realizing it, pushing the limits of what safety looked like for my parents.

What felt like growth to me required courage from them.
What felt like curiosity to me required trust from them.
They were learning, slowly, how to let their daughter step outward, while still holding on with love. I was learning how to move forward without breaking the bonds that held me.
My mother became the quiet balance in that transition — understanding both the protectiveness of a parent and the restlessness of a growing daughter. She held space with patience, allowing expansion without fracture. I share this context not to explain or justify my choices, but to place them honestly. Every step I took was taken from within a family rooted in faith, discipline, and care. The story that

follows is story of expansion within love, of learning how far one can go while still remaining connected.

My grandparents gave me confidence.
My parents gave me discipline.
My siblings gave me grounding.
Together, they formed the soil from which I grew.
If you are reading this from a different culture or a different generation, I ask you to read what follows with th
is in mind: growth does not always look dramatic. Sometimes it looks like quiet persistence within a carefully held world.
This was mine.
And from here, the journey begins.

CONTENTS

Temple Bells & Balcony Dreams 3

The Years of Fire and Fog.. 15

The Shift from Surviving to Thriving................................ 29

When the World Said No, the Dream Whispered-YES 43

PhD: The New Beginnings... 57

Claiming My Seat at the Table....................................... 69

Stepping into the Unknown... 81

Rising to the Moment 93

The Work Before the Flight to Unknown........................ 103

Postdoctoral Life: Learning to Live Between Worlds 111

Molecules, Motherhood, and the Cost of Continuity...... 123

The Rise After the Pause... 143

Keeping the Light Alive and Building Beyond Myself 157

Just absorb

Temple Bells & Balcony Dreams

(Childhood in Unnao, Nana-Nani's home, innocence, early impressions of doctors, rituals, self-belief)

"तत्त्वमसि।", Chandogya Upanishad 6.8.7

You are That.
You are not small.
You are not accidental.
You already carry within you what you are searching for.
The journey is not about becoming someone else,
It is about remembering who you already are.

I didn't grow up with pressure.
I grew up with prayers, poojas, poori, poise, and the poetry of simplicity.
My life was not designed to impress., It was designed to nurture, to observe, to feel. And it did. Every morning, every mantra, every meal, every mirror-talk with God was part of an extraordinary childhood I didn't know was extraordinary at the time.

Befikri: My Greatest Privilege

Being befikra, carefree, was the best thing that ever happened to me.
There was no scoreboard hanging over my head. No lectures about marks. No demand to top the class.
That freedom gave me space to breathe, explore, and laugh without guilt.
And because no one at home expected me to become anything extraordinary, I never felt jealousy, never held grudges. I was never in a race. That kind of environment made me content, even fulfilled, at an age when most children learn to compete before they learn to understand themselves.

My Royal Life Without a Crown

I lived with my Nana and Nani, and they raised me like a true princess, not by spoiling me, but by shielding me from the weight of societal expectations.
During festivals, especially on Navratri, my Nani would treat me like I was sacred. I was never asked for anything. Never taught house chores. I was allowed to simply be.
They never once questioned "Why educate a girl so much?", They were far ahead of their time. Progressive, kind, and full of clarity.
For them, I wasn't "just a girl." I was potential.

A Home Built on Humanity

Our house was filled with people from all walks of life. My Nana's deep roots in the villages of Unnao, combined with his connections in the city, meant that on any day, our living room could host a high court judge or a village farmer, or both. It was the perfect setting to witness the grounded and inclusive worldview that quietly shaped my upbringing.

Doctors rented clinics on our first floor. There was a pathology lab, X-ray center, pharmacy stores, and every day I saw patients come and go. Some healed, some crying, some forever gone. Just across the street was the district hospital.

For me, watching the flow of life and death, of hope and despair, of recovery and grief, became normal. But I didn't realize then, that I was being primed by the divine.
I didn't decide to do something big. I was just absorbing everything.
Silently. Constantly.

Saraswati Shishu Mandir: My Sacred School

From nursery to 8th grade, I studied at Saraswati Shishu Mandir, A.B. Nagar, Unnao, Uttar Pradesh, India. It was a school that didn't just shape my mind, it shaped my spirit.
Every morning began with Pratah Smaran, Saraswati Vandana, Shanti Mantra, and Bhajan Path. These daily rituals planted a deep faith within me, so deep, it still grounds me.

I was never the class topper. But I was beloved.
Teachers trusted me. They would write my name down for school programs without even asking. Singing, dancing, debating. I became Vandana Pramukh, Utsav Pramukh and

Senapati. Not because I was great, but because my sincerity stood out.

The Power of Being "Average" and Still Admired

I didn't win because I was the best. I won because I showed up, again and again, with my whole heart. My classmates liked me. I had no rivalries. No fears. Just presence.
And that's when I learned one of life's biggest lessons early: You don't need to compete to lead. You can lead by simply being real.

I remember the tours with teachers and classmates. The school events, interschool song competitions, debates, and patriotic dances. Those tiny victories, , standing first in a poem recitation, winning a debate round, , gave me a quiet confidence that would follow me around the world.

A World Beyond the Classroom

The best classroom I ever sat in wasn't made of four walls, whiteboards, or lecture slides.
It was the India trip with my Nana and Nani.
It was the window seat of a crowded train.
It was the shared thali in a stranger's home.
It was temple bells, dusty roads and spiritual chants echoing in the Himalayan air to Kanyakumari breeze.
With them, I traveled across the length and breadth of this country. Gujarat, Rajasthan, Madhya Pradesh, Andhra Pradesh, Tamil Nadu, Uttarakhand, Nepal, Punjab, Maharashtra.

From the sacred Jyotirlingas to the holy Char Dham, I saw India not through textbooks, but through temples, train windows, local accents, barefoot walks, and kind eyes.

These travels did not earn me degrees.
But they taught me the skills no university can teach.

They taught me how to talk to strangers with respect, how to listen, how to navigate unfamiliar places, how to sleep without a fan, how to eat what's served with a smile, how to share space with ten others, how to wake up before sunrise for temple darshan, how to wait, and how to be grateful even when you have very little.
They taught me faith, in people, in divine timing, and in myself.

They taught me, culture, not as a subject, but as a lived truth.
They taught me adaptability,that home is not a place, but a mindset.
And most of all, they taught me that humility is the greatest wisdom.
In those journeys, I learned what no entrance exam can measure:
How to be human.

So, to every student reading this, , don't just chase marks.
Chase meaning.
Step out of your comfort zone.
Speak to people outside your world.
Travel if you can, , even if it's just on foot to the next town.
The real world is waiting to educate you, for free.
Because one day, it won't be your rank, your percentage, or your medal that sets you apart.
It will be your grit, your grace, your groundedness.
It will be your real-world intelligence that helps you rise and stay there.

My Relationship with God

God wasn't a figure on a wall.
God was my friend.

I spoke to God every day. I shared secrets. I imagined my future. Sometimes I stood in front of the mirror and gave speeches, not to classmates, but to an imaginary auditorium.
At every temple, I felt seen.
At every bell, I felt heard.
And somehow, I just knew that He was listening.

Mirror Talks and Diaries

One of the quietest, most profound gifts my Nana gave me was the habit of journaling.
Whenever we traveled, , which we did often, , he would hand me a notebook and say,
"Write everything you see. Everything you feel."
And I did. Diligently. Sincerely.
I wasn't trying to be a writer. I wasn't even aware I was developing a habit.

I was just capturing the world through my eyes, with wide wonder and honest words.
Later, when neighbors or relatives came to ask my Nana about temple routes, yatra schedules, train timings, or darshan queues, he would often say,
"Ask her. She notes everything."
I loved that moment.

Not because I was being praised, but because I was being trusted.
Unknowingly, I was building the foundation of public speaking.
I was training in memory recall.
I was growing a quiet confidence to speak in front of others.
To explain, narrate, and connect.
I didn't know I was learning storytelling.
I didn't know I was learning observation, articulation, and empathy, all the things that make a speaker great.

And when no one was around, I practiced again, in front of the mirror.

I would imagine myself as someone important.
A speaker. A teacher. A guest of honor.
I would hold my brush like a mic and rehearse speeches in my mind.
Sometimes I would pretend I was being interviewed.
Other times, I would smile like I had won an award.
There was no one clapping. No one watching.
But I was watching myself.
And that was enough.
It was a play. A child's harmless fantasy.
But somewhere deep within, , I believed it.
Not in a loud, arrogant way. But in a silent, powerful way.
Some part of me felt:
"Yes, I can be this. Maybe I already am."

And maybe that is why it came true.
Because so many dreams don't start on big stages.
They start in front of quiet mirrors.
In little notebooks.
In whispered rehearsals.
That's where we plant the seed, , and life finds a way to water it.

Watching the World from the Balcony

My favorite pastime was watching the highway traffic from our balcony. Buses, trucks, honking cars, were the background score to my daydreams.
Below us, real life happened: hospitals, people, pain, politics, relatives, rumors. I was absorbing everything, from courtroom discussions to village disputes, medical consultations to spiritual conversations.
High to low. Urban to rural. Science to faith.
It all lived in our home. And I was its quiet observer.

Words That Stayed with Me

One day, my Nana's name appeared in the newspaper. He had organized a -Samuhik Vivah, a mass marriage ceremony. When I showed it to him excitedly, he said something I've never forgotten:
"A person's name comes in the newspaper for only two reasons: 1). They've done something very good; OR 2). something very bad."
That line stayed with me.
Because it wasn't just about reputation.
It was about impact on humanity. About living meaningfully.

When You Are Seen, You Learn to See Others

My Nana-Nani made me feel seen every day. And in that love, I learned how to see others, , not their success, but their soul.
They taught me empathy not by words, but by action. They helped anyone they could , within their means , and I watched, quietly absorbing, again.
Today, I volunteer with Sewa International in the USA, and the seed of that seva was planted right here, in a small-town home, where giving was just life.

Reflections:

Freedom from pressure is a privilege. If you have it, use it to explore who you are.
You don't need to be a topper to be trusted or respected. Sincerity is seen by those who matter.

Travel, rituals, and faith give your soul a foundation. Never underestimate their power.

Helping others, listening, watching , are silent forms of leadership.

Your childhood shapes you in invisible ways. Embrace it. Celebrate it. Heal it if needed.
Some childhoods are shaped by ambition. Others by love. Mine was shaped by presence, , by being seen, trusted, and allowed to grow without fear. Before I understood success, I learned belonging.
Looking back, those early years were not ordinary. They were divinely orchestrated, carefully crafted to shape me, not through achievement, but through alignment.

I wasn't a prodigy. I wasn't a topper. I didn't win medals for marks. But I was surrounded by unseen abundance, of wisdom, grace, values, and love. I was nurtured not by pressure but by presence. My Nana and Nani were my world, and through them, I learnt how a child becomes strong not by control, but by belief.

I didn't understand it then, but the temple bells, the school stage, the quiet train journeys across India, the smell of ghee in Nani's kitchen, and the old men discussing philosophy in my home, were all teaching me how to carry myself with dignity. How to respect everyone, from high court judges to farmers. How to stay grounded no matter how high you dream.
People often believe that only toppers can do something big in life. But I was average in academics. Still, I was never average in dreams.
What made the difference?
I was seen. I was heard. I was believed in.

That kind of childhood builds a quiet kind of confidence. One that doesn't always show up in exam scores, , but shows up when life gets hard, when failures come, when the world

doubts you. It's a confidence that says, "Maybe I'm not extraordinary yet. But I'm capable. Just watch."
So, if you are reading this and feel like you're just an "average student" ... please know this:

You are not behind. You are being prepared.
You don't need permission to dream.
You just need someone who believes in you,, and until you find them, believe in yourself.
I didn't realize it, but the seed of my courage was planted during these years. Not through textbooks,, but through life itself.

Questions for the Reader:

- Where did you feel most seen as a child?
- What invisible gifts did your childhood give you?
- How can you honor that part of yourself today?

Learn. Rise. Enjoy

The Years of Fire and Fog

(Transition to Kanpur, adolescence, loss, failure, resilience, early sparks of confidence)

अणोरणीयान् महतो महीयान्, आत्माऽस्य जन्तोर्निहितो गुहायाम्।
तमक्रतुः पश्यति वीतशोको, धातुप्रसादान्महिमानमीशम्— Katha Upanishad-1.2.20

Your potential may be invisible today. But with the right exposure and guidance, it can grow far beyond what anyone currently sees.

In 1999, things Changed.

I left behind the cocoon of love and emotional freedom I had known at my Nana–Nani's home and moved into my parents' house in Kanpur. It wasn't just a shift in location. It was a shift in atmosphere, rhythm, and expectation. The world felt suddenly quieter, more contained.

The girl who once danced freely in temple courtyards, watched highway traffic from balconies, and spoke to God like a close friend now had to learn to be careful, to lower her voice, and to fit into a life shaped by routine rather than imagination.

Yet life in Kanpur was not unpleasant. It was ordinary. Predictable. Rooted in the realities of a middle-class Indian household at the turn of the millennium.
I studied in a government public school. My days followed a familiar pattern: early mornings, uniforms neatly pressed, school bags packed in a rush. Afternoons were spent returning home hungry, dropping our bags on the floor, and waiting for lunch.

My mother was the emotional center of the house (She still is). She cooked - kheer on some days, aloo sabzi, nimona and puri on others, kachoris when time allowed. She had a way of making food feel like reassurance. She would wait for us every day, listening to our footsteps, watching the street quietly.

By evening, the house filled with noise again like bird's chirping. Girls giggling, conversations overlapping, doors opening and closing. My younger sister, Niharika, and I talked constantly about school, friends, nothing important and everything at once.

Life moved in loops.

Morning school.

Afternoon meals.

Evening wandering within the house.

Helping younger siblings, doing house chores.

Nighttime television, shared glances, quiet tiredness.

Sometimes we walked to nearby temples, especially Siddhi Vinayak. Sometimes we visited Dadi's house. Occasionally, we traveled to Unnao, revisiting fragments of my earlier life. My father often went to Anandeshwar Temple and returned with small treats- Jalebi, Dhokla, chaat, gajak, samosas- unexpected pleasures that broke the monotony.

It was a simple life.

Not exciting.

Not tragic.

Just steady.

Learning to Belong in a New City - Kanpur

The transition from being a protected granddaughter to a disciplined daughter wasn't smooth. At my Nana–Nani's home, emotions flowed freely. In Kanpur, emotions were managed quietly.

This wasn't about right or wrong. It was about the difference. On my father's side, expectations followed the norms of that generation. Daughters were guided carefully, protected until

marriage. Sons carried symbolic importance. Education was encouraged- but only to a certain point.
At the time, our family consisted of my parents, my sister Niharika, and me, living in a modest two-bedroom rented place. In 2000, my sister Vidhi was born. In 2004, my brother arrived.

Despite the significant age gaps, I shared a deep bond with my siblings. I became responsible early, helping my mother, watching over infant and toddlers, learning patience before I fully understood it.
Our household was religious. Rituals shaped our days. Faith was not loud, but it was constant. No one intended to restrict me. The structure came from concern, care, and love.
Still, adapting took time.

From Dreams to Duties

Like many families, including mine, a girl's future felt clearly outlined: be a good daughter, then a good daughter-in-law, a good wife. Education was permitted, but ambition had invisible limits.

Within this framework, my parents made a quietly bold choice. They allowed me to study science.
I was the first girl in the family to take science. At the same time, I was learning how to manage a growing household.

When my youngest sister was born just 65 days before my Class 10 board exams, I studied beside my mother in the hospital room. Books on the one hand, responsibility in the other. I was handing multiple responsibilities: my mom and

infant sister in the hospital, household when I came back from hospital.
I scored second division in my Class 10 exams. It reflected the confusion and exhaustion of that period.

The Image of a Perfect, Obedient Girl

As I said earlier, life at home was quiet, disciplined, and predictable.
I was an obedient girl, an "average" student, at least that is how I appeared to others, even to myself.
I did not know what my abilities were.
And my parents did not know either.

Not because they lacked faith in me, but because there was nothing in my scorecard that signaled exceptional academic promise to them. A report card was the only way to know a kid's intelligence at that time, perhaps now too.
Even the idea that I might pursue a master's degree felt uncertain to my parents.
I did what I was told.
I wore what I was given.
I went where I was taken.
I was a *good daughter, even the perfect one*.

So good that no one imagined I would make my choices in life or chart a path that had not already been drawn for me.
But the truth that, I understood much later was that the ability was always there in me.

If it had not been, I would not have become a scientist.

The gap was not intelligence.
"THE GAP WAS ENVIRONMENT and EXPOSURE"
I grew up without any academic role models around me.
Without access to an intellectually stimulating environment around me.

Without mentors who could recognize my potential before it learned how to speak for itself.
There was no one to listen to, no one to guide, no one to help me imagine what was possible.
"And when exposure and imagination is missing, ambition rarely takes root".

I knew how to become an ideal daughter, an ideal future daughter-in-law.
But no one told me that I had the capacity to become a scientist.
What I understand now is this:
Talent is often silent.
It requires guidance to find its voice.
This belief, born from lived experience, later became the foundation of my work:
With the right exposure, the right mentorship, and the right encouragement, many students can discover abilities they were never taught to recognize in themselves.

When Everything Collapsed

Class 12 broke me.
Both my Nana Ji and Dadaji passed away during this time. My Nana-my emotional anchor- was diagnosed with liver

cancer. We took him to SGPGIMS in Lucknow, hoping for answers. There were none.

He was brought back to Kanpur in a small hospital.
I watched him fade slowly.
One day, I clipped his nails while he lay in a coma. His skin turned yellow. His hands were cold. Tears rolled down his closed eyes because of the cancer pain.
After that night, he never woke up again
That moment quietly ended my childhood.
I was in mental shock for months if not years which I could never share with anyone.

I failed my Class 12 board exams—not because I wasn't capable, but because I didn't know how to process grief, people around me, study effectively at the same time, or ask for help. I was overwhelmed and unprepared.
Still, something shifted inside me. I didn't know it then.

Learning to Stand

I restarted my 12th grade— not with confidence, but with a heavy heart. I reopened my textbooks quietly, almost shamefully, as if I had to negotiate with my own disappointment before turning each page. Going back to school again felt humbling in a way I was not prepared for. There was sadness, there was self-doubt, and there was the silent fear of being judged. I joined a simple local coaching center with only a few teachers — nothing prestigious, nothing impressive to announce socially. But in that modest classroom, something shifted. They did not just teach subjects; teachers noticed me. They taught me how to study structurally — how to break down concepts, plan revision cycles, analyze mistakes, and build consistency. For the first time, preparation felt less emotional and more strategic. That phase rebuilt not just my knowledge, but my discipline. I was studying to rebuild myself.

I passed Class 12 in my second attempt, again in the second division. But this time, I felt something new: confidence. Not pride. Not victory. Just belief.
I realized that failing didn't make me incapable. It meant I had never been taught the right method.

Becoming Strong Quietly

After 12th grade, I was enrolled in **B.Sc. Life Sciences at A. N. D. Mahila Mahavidyalaya**.
For the first time in my life, I was reading **textbooks in English**.

It was a major transition. Until then, my learning had been largely Hindi-medium. Now, every page demanded extra effort. I always kept a dictionary beside me, reading a word in English, then carefully writing its Hindi meaning above it with a pencil in the textbooks. Studying took twice the time. Sometimes more. Much of my energy went not into memorizing concepts- but simply **understanding what the book was saying**.

It was slow. Exhausting. Often discouraging.
But I didn't quit.
Around the same time, another parallel reality was unfolding at home.

In families like mine, this age- early twenties- is traditionally seen as the *right time* for a girl's marriage. I was studying, but my father also kept a quiet watch for "good boys" within his circle- friends, acquaintances, families with similar values. Discussions about my future would surface naturally during family conversations.
This was not pressure.
It was preparation.

Education and marriage were not viewed as opposites. They moved side by side- one visible in classrooms, the other quietly shaping expectations at home. This was common in families like ours, where a daughter is lovingly trained not just to succeed, but to **adjust**.

A girl, especially a first daughter, is raised to become an *ideal bahu* more than an ideal individual.
My parents prepared me the best way they knew how.
They taught me how to sit, composed and attentive.
How to speak remaining, measured and respectful.
How to listen carefully and care deeply.

They taught me rituals, household responsibilities, emotional restraint, and adaptability- everything needed to fit into any family I might one day walk into as a bahu.
This training did not come from limitation.
It came from love, lived experience, and generational wisdom.

I absorbed it sincerely.
At the same time, I was learning something else- quietly, unintentionally- through science textbooks, long study

hours, and small academic victories. I was learning how to think, how to persist, how to improve through method rather than luck.
Two versions of me were growing side by side.
One learning how to belong to a family.
Another beginning to belong to herself.
Then my brother was born.

The joy was unmistakable. Sweets were distributed. Relatives visited. Celebrations filled the house. I observed it all quietly- not with resentment, but with awareness. I began to understand how differently expectations operate, even within love.

I responded not with rebellion, but responsibility.
I loved to help raise my siblings-two bundles of joy. I supported my mother in house chores. Sometimes, I even supported my father in his machinery store.

Festivals remained moments of happiness. **Holi and Diwali** were major events, , new clothes, mithai, crackers, laughter filling the house. We celebrated other festivals; Dussehra, Navratri. I enjoyed going to fairs, eating GolGappe, riding on the giant wheel. **Sundays** were reserved for relatives, special and shared meals, long conversations, familiar faces, and familiar roles.

Space at home was limited. I had no study desk. No room of my own. I studied in stolen hours of early mornings and late nights, once my siblings had fallen asleep. It was a very different setup from most college students, but it was the only one available to me.

During this time, a college friend taught me something life-changing: **how to study any topic in english**.
Read and write repeatedly until you master each thing about that topic.
That was when my scores began to change.
First sixty percent.
Then the first division.
Then consistency.

My mother quietly paid for my entrance-exam forms from her household savings. I prepared while completing my undergraduate final-year studies, balancing home responsibilities and academic ambition without ever naming it as ambition.
I wasn't chasing success yet.
I was learning, slowly, steadily, to believe in myself.

Reflection:

This chapter isn't about setbacks. It's about **growing up without a manual**.
Nothing dramatic happened here. No overnight success, no rebellion, no big breakthrough. Just school, family, failure, festivals, routines, and responsibility.
And that's exactly the point.

Most lives aren't built in highlight reels. They're built in **repeat mode**.
Same school. Same house. Same expectations. Same doubts.
When life feels boring, stuck, or slow, it usually means something inside you is being shaped - **quietly**.

If your life feels repetitive, underwhelming, behind others, emotionally heavy, invisible ...nothing is "wrong" with you.

- What if your current "ordinary" phase is actually your training ground?
- What if nothing has gone wrong, only deeper roots are being formed?
- What if your struggles are not delays, but *filters*?

You're not late. You're not broken. You're **building something that doesn't show up on Instagram**. Some people grow fast and burn out. Some people grow slowly and last long.
You don't need to have it all figured out. You just need to **keep becoming**. And that's enough.

Questions for reader:

- Have you ever confused lack of support with lack of talent?
- Who helped you in small, everyday ways that mattered more than big advice?
- If success wasn't the goal, what would you still want to become?

Exposure Expands Identity

The Shift from Surviving to Thriving

(First-First, Jhansi, New life, hostel life)

यो वै भूमा तत्सुखम्, नाल्पे सुखमस्ति — *Chandogya Upanishad 7.23.1*

You were never meant to stay small.
Real growth begins when you choose a bigger version of yourself.

On the last day of my final BSc III exam, I had a small accident right before the exam time. After the exam, I came back home in pain.

Sometimes life takes a turn in ways we can't predict. A small accident left me injured, but in hindsight, it was a divine nudge. As I sat at home, nursing my foot, I had the time and space to prepare for something I had been quietly dreaming about- entrance exams for postgraduate studies.

During this time, my close family friend coached me in cracking the entrance exams for a few weeks. For the first time, I was taught the actual mechanics of cracking competitive exams:

Time management for MCQs.
Understanding examiners' expectations.
Strategic preparation.
It wasn't a lack of knowledge that had held me back all those years. It was a lack of exposure and technique. That's when I understood the power of it.

Cracking the Entrance Exams

I gave entrance tests for Pharmacy, Microbiology, and Forensic Science, the last one at Lucknow University. And by God's grace, I cleared all three exams. That moment was huge for an average academic girl. I was full of gratitude towards the Almighty. It was a signal that I have some substance inside me.

Although my dad was more inclined that I should study in Kanpur, I chose Forensic Science at Bundelkhand University, Jhansi - a decision that would shape the rest of my life.

My mother packed me lunch as if she were packing reassurance itself, extra puri-kachori folded carefully, sabzi wrapped tightly so it wouldn't spill, a small container of sweets "just in case." She laid out my clothes the night before, smoothing the fabric with her hands, as if touch alone could protect me once I was gone. Between packing bags, she whispered blessings, , half aloud, half to herself, , prayers meant to travel farther than she ever had.

My Nani came all the way from Unnao just for this moment. She didn't bring advice or instructions. She came to place **Vijay Tilak** on my forehead, her fingers steady, her eyes moist. It was her way of saying: *You are not leaving alone. You are carrying us with you.*

That morning, the house felt heavier than usual, not with fear, but with significance. No one said it out loud, but everyone understood: this was not an ordinary departure.

This wasn't just a girl leaving for higher education.
This was something unprecedented.

A middle-class family sending its **first daughter**, its **first science student**, beyond the familiar boundaries of the city. A girl stepping out not for marriage, not for obligation, but for education. For the possibility. For a future that no one in the family had lived before.

Suitcases stood quietly in the corner, but what they held went far beyond clothes and books. They carried hope, hesitation, pride, and generations of silent wishes. My parents didn't have the language to call it courage, but that's what it was.

In that moment, no banners were raised, no speeches made. Yet a revolution was unfolding,quietly, respectfully, without resistance. A revolution that did not shout but walked forward anyway.

I wasn't just crossing city limits.
I was crossing expectations.
And behind me stood a family that may not have fully understood where I was going, but chose, bravely, to let me go.

I remember eating dosa with my father at a restaurant near Elite Chauraha in Jhansi after my counseling. He didn't say much, but I could read his emotions: pride, anxiety, hope. For a man carrying the weight of societal expectations, this was a bold, almost rebellious move: sending his daughter alone to study in another city.

However, we both did not know at that moment that things would change between us soon.

A New World: Jhansi

Jhansi wasn't just a city. It was fresh air. For the first time, I wasn't someone's daughter, sister, or niece. I was just... me.

I was in a hostel with eight girls: Pooja Gupta, Mamta Singh, Bindu Singh, Monika Gupta, Vanshree, and Nitu Singh, all from different departments, and a temple right in front, , as if the universe was watching over us. My roommate, Pooja Gupta, became my best friend. I made friends for life in Jhansi, Keerti Srivastava was one of them. These girls were all brilliant, all of them the topper of their department, and suddenly, I wasn't the odd one out. I was one of them.
Our lives had rhythm:

Study from 9 PM to 3 AM
Wake up by 8 AM, attend classes
Return by 4 PM, nap
Wake by 8 PM, tea, dinner, and back to study

No shopping malls. No cafes. I didn't even have that much money to spend. Our parties were visits to Kaimasan Mata Temple, Ram Raja Temple in Orchha, and the Datiya Siddh Peeth. Our luxuries were patties and coffee at the local medical college. And yet, I never felt so rich, because I had purpose, direction, and sisterhood.

Finding My Voice, Finding Myself

For someone raised in a restrictive and disciplined setup, freedom was both thrilling and intimidating. Jhansi gave me the space to:

Learn how to make friends
How to be in a co-education model
Groom myself
Laugh without judgment
Study without distraction

I had never stayed in a hostel before. I didn't even know how to share space or be vulnerable. But this space, this life, was preparing me for the future I had only dared to imagine. Academically, I soared at Bundelkhand University. I set my eyes on a new goal: UGC-JRF.

With little money and no online resources, I photocopied books, took extensive handwritten notes, and spent 5+ hours in the university library daily. My nights belonged to my studies. My strategy? Learn the syllabus like a mantra. Every page, every topic, not just read, but ingrained. My days were for survival. But my spirit? My spirit was growing wings.

My professor sent me to CFSL Chandigarh, where I interacted with scientists and directors. My confidence skyrocketed. Then, I presented a poster at the university symposium and won second prize. My dreams were no longer whispers. They were declarations. I topped my department in the final year. All flying colors.

Thesis, Mentors, and Meaning

My M.Sc. thesis, "Comparison of Blood Group Detection Methods for 25-Year-Old Blood Stains," was conducted at CFSL/CBI, New Delhi. I met renowned forensic experts like Dr. Bibha Rani Ray (Ex-Director of CFSL/CBI, New Delhi), Dr. Asha Srivastava (Ex-Director of CFSL/CBI, New Delhi), and Dr. Harsh Sharma (Ex-Director of SCFSL, Bhopal). They weren't just professionals. They became mentors, life coaches, and divine connections.
Every trip between Jhansi and Delhi felt like a step into a wider world.

I finished my MSc thesis in CFSL/CBI New Delhi and came back to Bundelkhand University campus. Now I had limited time to finish everything in MSc.

I knew home didn't have the right environment to prepare for UGC-JRF. So, I decided to stay in Jhansi for two more weeks. So, right after my final exams, I packed up everything and returned to Kanpur for just one week, only to head straight into the UGC-JRF exam.

My parents and me

In my extended family, no girl before me had pursued higher education beyond what was expected. No woman had built a career shaped by research, travel, mentors, or professional networks. Such possibilities did not belong to our vocabulary. I was a middle-class daughter stepping beyond imagination, not intention.
It was not rebellion that unsettled the ground beneath us — it was unfamiliarity.

Even now, there may be girls in my family who are not walking this path — perhaps because they do not yet know it exists. Between my M.Sc. and Ph.D., while I was quietly assembling the scaffolding of my future, my relationship with my father moved through storms — some spoken, many silent.
Not from lack of love.
because there was lot of love.

He was a protective father carrying three daughters, financial caution, conservative family pressure and the gaze of society. Each time I traveled alone across India in pursuit of education, What felt like expansion to me felt like crossing boundaries to him. My courage translated into his fear. My independence registered as his loss of fatherly control. And yet, despite all of it, my parents let me go for higher education to different cities.

I was stretching the boundaries he had built out of care.
He was holding them because letting go felt like failure.
My mother stood between us — absorbing friction, translating tension into patience, allowing two generations to renegotiate trust, redefining the girl's designation in the family like us.

This, I believe, is the burden of the first torchbearer — to walk ahead of tradition and quietly begin changing it.

Only later did I understand as I was learning to become independent, my father was learning how to parent an independent daughter. The movement from protection to permission was gradual.

This was not defiance.
It was inheritance shifting.

A quiet recalibration of what daughters are allowed to become — where love does not diminish but learns to widen. And perhaps that is what *Tat Tvam Asi* truly means in real life — not becoming someone else but slowly recognizing that you were always meant to become yourself.

Reflection:

These two years, 2007 to 2009, were nothing short of transformational. For the first time in my life, I wasn't surviving. I was thriving.

I discovered:
My intelligence
My voice
My worth
My courage
My goals
My method
My mentors
I stopped hiding.
I stopped doubting.

I wasn't just a girl with dreams anymore. I was a girl taking action.
Jhansi prepared me for the world. To walk alone, study with obsession, trust myself, and build meaningful relationships.

It was where I found my true self, not just the student, but the woman I would carry into the rest of my life.
And all of it began... because I got the appropriate environment and time to dream during my BSc time.

"When life takes something from you, it often gives you something greater in return: the chance to become who you were always meant to be."

These two years changed my life.

From a girl who once studied in government girls' school to a postgraduate topper. From crying quietly in crowded rooms to studying under candlelight in peace. From doubt to devotion. From being told I couldn't prove that I could.

Jhansi made me brave. I found my voice. I mastered the syllabus. I made lifelong friendships. I launched a dream.

So if you're standing at the edge of leaving home, unsure of what lies beyond the city you grew up in, remember this:
Sometimes your destiny lives in a place you've never been. Sometimes a stranger becomes your mentor. Sometimes your failure is your entry ticket.
You are not running away. You are stepping into your truth.

A Message for Readers

If you're reading this while feeling lost, overwhelmed, or quietly behind everyone else, pause for a second.

You are not late.
You are not weak.
You are not broken.

Most of us were never taught *how* to grow. We were taught, only *what* to achieve. No one explained the rules of the game, the techniques, the exposure, or the inner work. So, when things feel hard, you assume it's because *you* are lacking.
You're not.

Sometimes all it takes is:

- One mentor
- One new environment
- One chance to step away from expectations
- One moment of courage that feels terrifying but true

Growth doesn't always look glamorous. Often, it looks like studying alone while others party. Saying no when everyone expects yes. Choosing uncertainty over comfort. Leaving home not because you don't love it, but because you need to find yourself.

Here's something no algorithm will tell you:
Your confidence will not arrive before action. It comes *after*.

Your voice gets stronger only when you use it, imperfectly.
Your path may scare your parents, confuse society, and isolate you, but that doesn't mean it's wrong.
If you're an "average" student right now, remember this:
Average beginnings do not predict ordinary endings.

And if you feel like you're growing quietly, unseen, good.

That's how real revolutions begin.

Not loud.
Not viral.
But honest.
Focused.
Relentless.
Keep going.
Your future self is already proud of you.

Questions for the Reader:

- What part of yourself are you holding back to keep others comfortable?
- Whose fear are you carrying, yours, or someone else's?
- What would your life look like if you trusted your inner calling?
- Are you growing quietly, or waiting for permission to grow?

Persist Beyond Labels

When the World Said No, the Dream Whispered-YES

(Mentors, blessing and New Delhi)

भिद्यते हृदयग्रन्थिः, छिद्यन्ते सर्वसंशयाः — ***Mundaka Upanishad 2.2.8***

The knots in your heart — the fears, labels, and limiting beliefs — can break. When they do, doubt loses its power over you.

By 2009, something shifted, not just around me, but within me.

I had just completed my MSc in Forensic Science and returned to my home in Kanpur. On paper, I had done everything right: a postgraduate degree, decent academic standing, and was at what society comfortably labeled as “marriageable age.” But inside, I was carrying questions far bigger than any syllabus could answer.
I had no job.
No salary.

No certainty, whether, personal or professional.
Only a restlessness that refused to settle.
Before leaving Jhansi, I had one final academic stop: **State Forensic Science Laboratory (SFSL), Bhopal**. It wasn’t part of the curriculum. It wasn’t planned. But it became a **divine appointment**.

I went to meet **Dr. Harsh Sharma**, a renowned forensic scientist, and unknowingly, one of the most important mentors of my life.
Dr. Sharma didn’t just show me a lab.
He opened a world.

He introduced me to senior scientists and professors like **Dr. Satapathy**, Dean of Bhopal Medical College. He invited me to observe a live crime scene. He introduced me to his family. Their warmth and acceptance showed me something I had never witnessed before: Mentorship was not transactional. It was relational.

He saw something in me I hadn't yet learned to see in myself. And when someone does that, it plants a quiet strength that never really leaves you. This is the power of true mentor. During my dissertation at **CFSL/CBI, New Delhi**, Dr. Sharma invited me to attend a national forensic conference in Agra. Because of his referral, my registration fee was waived. We traveled together by train, talking about science, ethics, life, and purpose.

I remember sitting by the window, watching fields rush past, thinking:
I am standing at the edge of something big.
And yet, back home, reality felt very different.
I was still a girl with no job.
No income.
And a growing chorus around me saying:
"Shaadi ki baat karni chahiye."
"Age ho rahi hai."
"Kya fayda hua itna padhne ka?"
The contrast was painful.

In Agra, I stood among India's top forensic experts, Dr. V.K. Sehgal, Dr. Ranjeet Singh, Surender Baisoya, and many more. Brilliant minds. And not once did I feel small.
That's the power of sincere preparation.
Authenticity commands respect.

I didn't have the language for it then, but I was having an epiphany:
When you are honest, humble, and hardworking, the universe responds, not immediately, but **precisely**.

Back in Kanpur, that inner expansion collided with social expectation.

I had taken the **UGC-JRF exam** in June. By August, the pressure returned,stronger, louder.
This time, something inside me refused to collapse.
So, I turned fear into motion.
I began visiting internet cafés, sometimes spending hours collecting email IDs of scientists across forensic institutes. I wrote to them. I called them. I asked for advice, opportunities,anything.
Some were surprised.
Some were confused.
Many were kind.
I was no longer waiting to be rescued.
I was building my own ladder.

Once again, Dr. Harsh Sharma became a rung on that ladder. He referred me to **SFSL Rohini, New Delhi**, for a contract position as Scientific Associate.
I packed a bag.
Took a sleeper-class waiting ticket.
And went.
The interview happened.
I was selected.
My first job.
₹5,000 per month.
No work, no pay.

In Delhi, I had **no extra money**. Just enough for rent, food, and commute. I never thought about clothes, brands, malls,

or outings. McDonald's, shopping, lipsticks, , those worlds did not exist for me.
My hunger was different.

While girls around me were shopping for tops and accessories, I was shopping for **books, forms, and exam syllabi**. My weekends were spent either buried in notes or quietly at my friend Rajbala's house,resting, recalibrating, returning to my books.
I was hungry.
Very hungry.
Not for luxury,but for **becoming**.
I didn't even know what I was hungry for exactly. I just knew it was something big. Something beyond my surroundings. That hunger has stayed with me all my life, and it has paid me back generously.

At SFSL, I trained under experts like **Paliwal Sir** and **A.K. Srivastava**, working in the DNA Fingerprinting Unit. Real criminal cases passed through my hands,charred clothes, bones, baby clothes, fragments of unimaginable loss.
Every case broke me a little.
Every case built me more.
It taught me the fragility of life,and the weight of truth.
And then, quietly, life rewarded persistence.
I filled out the UGC-JRF form again. My **second attempt**. But I qualified it in my first attempt.

UGC–JRF (University Grants Commission – Junior Research Fellowship)

It is one of India's most prestigious national examinations, designed for students who aspire to pursue research and a PhD. The examination does not merely test academic knowledge; it evaluates analytical thinking, discipline, and research aptitude. Students who qualify for the JRF receive financial fellowship support, enabling them to focus on higher education and research without economic pressure.
For me, UGC–JRF was far more than an examination — it was a signal of the confidence that was gradually taking shape within me: that I was not merely someone who dreamed, but someone prepared to step into the world of research. I wasn't just preparing for an exam—I was preparing to **claim my worth**.
Even with limited hours, I committed at least two hours every day. I wasn't just preparing for an exam. , I was preparing to **claim my worth**.

One freezing December evening, Manish, my friend, called casually and said,
"UGC result is out."
I had no internet at home. I asked him to check my roll number.
There was a pause.
Then he said,
"You qualified."
Silence.
I asked two more friends to confirm. They did.
That night, I didn't sleep. My entire being buzzed with disbelief and joy.

All my well-wishers and family blessings paid off on that night.
The next morning, **A.K. Srivastava Sir distributed sweets** in the office.

“It feels like I cleared JRF,” he smiled.
At home, my parents celebrated quietly. And I stood taller than ever before.
Because I had done the unthinkable.
No coaching.
No internet.
No computer.
Hindi-medium background.
Second-division marks.
A failed 12th-grade memory that once haunted me.
Just relentless belief.

Breaking the Curse

For years, I had lived under a quiet, invisible label.
Average.
Second division.
Hindi-medium.
No coaching.
No guidance.
No pedigree.

It was a label that didn’t scream, it whispered. It followed me into classrooms, into exam halls, into family conversations. It shaped expectations before I even spoke. Somewhere along the way, I had started believing it, too.

There was a time when my academic life felt like a loop I could not escape. No matter how hard I worked, the outcome stayed the same. Second division again. Another reminder that maybe this was all I was meant to be. That loop had become a psychological prison, one that slowly convinces you that effort has a ceiling.

I wanted to break free, but I didn't know how.
Something began to crack during my B.Sc. years. Slowly. Quietly. Not dramatically. I didn't transform overnight. I just refused to stop walking. And when I cleared the UGC-JRF, that crack finally split open.

Clearing JRF was not just qualifying for an exam.
It was **breaking a generational belief system**.
It was telling my younger self, the girl who once looked at her marksheet with shame, that her story was not over. That intelligence is not measured by early performance. That potential does not expire because of one bad year or one failed exam.
That night, as I lay awake in my small Delhi room, I realized something profound:

The curse was never academic.
It was psychological.
It was the belief that "people like me" don't go far.
That "girls like me" should settle early.
That ambition beyond a certain point is arrogance.
And I had shattered that belief, not with privilege, but with persistence.
I had no safety net.

No certainty, either personal or professional.
No guarantee that this effort would even pay off.
There were days in Delhi when I counted money before buying vegetables. Days when I chose walking over buses to save fare. Days when I ate simple food, wore the same clothes, and said no to everything that wasn't essential.
But I never felt poor.
Because I was rich with direction.

I was hungry.
Hungry not for comfort, but for *becoming*.
I didn't know what that "big life" looked like yet. I just knew it wasn't limited to my current surroundings. And that hunger, rawness, relentlessness, and patience, has stayed with me even today.
That hunger changed everything.
It taught me that life does not reward brilliance alone.
It rewards **staying power**.
Clearing JRF gave me something that no salary ever could give me **permission**. Not from society, not from family, but from myself. Permission to dream without apology. Permission to step into rooms where I did not yet feel ready. Permission to imagine a future that did not resemble my past.
From that moment on, the label of "average" no longer belonged to me.

Not because I became extraordinary overnight but because I finally understood this:
Average does not mean incapable.
It only means the world hasn't seen your fire yet.
And fire, once lit, cannot be unseen.

Reflection:

What defines this chapter is not success, it is **the cost I was willing to pay before success was guaranteed**.
I was willing to:

- Step out of my family home without financial security
- Live on ₹5,000 a month
- Travel alone without certainty
- Delay marriage without clarity of "what next."
- Jump the fence of comfort, tradition, and approval

This was not a rebellion.
It was alignment.
I wasn't escaping my family.
I was answering myself.
UGC-JRF didn't just validate my intelligence, it freed me from the label of *average*. It taught me that hardship is not punishment. It is **tuition**.
And I paid it willingly.
Because somewhere deep inside, I knewI was meant for something bigger than survival.

Message to the Average Student

This book is titled **Tat Tvam Asi —You Are That**.
At this very time is where I first lived this quote- **Tat Tvam Asi — You Are That**.
To every student who feels ordinary, unsure, boxed in by family, finances, or fear:
You already have what you need.

Not confidence.
Not connections.
Not permission.

Capacity.

Do not arrest yourself with the handcuffs of:

- "People like us don't do that."
- "I'll choose something safe."
- "Let me think after marriage."

If you are 23, don't ask what will earn the fastest.
Ask what you can love enough to do for 40 years.
For me, it was science.
For you, it may be art, law, teaching, policy, or service.
Decide.
Imagine.
Move.
Once you do, the universe rearranges itself.
That is *Tat Tvam Asi*.
You are already that.
You just have to stop doubting it.

Questions for the Reader:

- What fence in your life are you afraid to jump, even though staying inside is shrinking you?
- What price are you avoiding paying, even though growth demands it?
- Are you choosing safety because it's right, or because it's familiar?
- If you trusted your capacity fully, what would you attempt next?

Discipline Builds Confidence

PhD: The New Beginnings

श्रद्धा-भक्त्या उपपन्ना यथा लभते ज्ञानम्-*Katha Upanishad 1.2.23*

Knowledge comes to the one who walks forward with faith and sincere effort.

Now that I had cleared UGC–JRF, a new journey began, one that felt both exhilarating and unsettling. For the first time in my life, I had a national-level academic validation in my hands. And yet, the question that echoed inside me was surprisingly simple and overwhelming:
What do I do with this now?

Delhi

After the initial high of qualifying for JRF, I began searching for a PhD advisor. I knocked on doors across JNU and Delhi University, meeting professors from different branches of life sciences. They were all accomplished in their own fields, but no one quite knew what to do with me.
I came from forensic science.
They came from molecular biology, biochemistry, and genetics.
I was floating between disciplines, academically qualified but intellectually homeless.
It was during this phase that **A.K. Srivastava Sir** gently redirected me.
"Go meet Dr. Anupama Raina at AIIMS," he said.
I did.

But life had other plans.
That day, Dr. Raina had left early. I waited for some time and eventually stepped out of the department. As I walked away, I noticed smoke rising from the mortuary nearby.
It was quiet. Still. Unsettling.
I stopped walking.

And in that moment, without logic, without planning, a voice rose from deep within me. Not dramatic. Not loud. But unmistakably clear.

"Do your PhD in life science. Not forensic science."

It wasn't a thought.

It wasn't reasoning.

It was a command.

Something inside me shifted permanently in that instant.

I didn't yet understand why, but I knew it was true.

That moment shaped everything that followed.

Back to Kanpur

I returned to Kanpur carrying this clarity quietly inside me. I continued speaking to people about PhD admissions, but one thing was now certain: **forensic science was not my future**.

I visited IIT Kanpur. I explored possibilities. Nothing aligned.

And then I made a decision that looked irrational from the outside.

I resigned from my job at SFSL, Rohini, New Delhi.

I had no confirmed admission.

No advisor.

No roadmap.

Only conviction.

Delhi no longer felt like my *aashiyana*.

I sat down with my parents and asked them to pause their groom-hunting efforts.

"God has brought me this far," I told them. "Let me walk the rest of the path."

For the first time, they agreed.

And then something remarkable happened, something that would repeat itself many times in my life.
When you step out with nothing but sincerity and courage, **life begins to meet you halfway**.
People appear.
Doors open.

A quiet guidance takes over.
That is the Universe responding, not to ambition, but to intention.

When your purpose is not ego-driven, but rooted in becoming something meaningful, logic alone stops being enough. You begin to move with the blessings of your parents, your grandparents, your ancestors, your entire bloodline walking with you.
If you ever find yourself in a moment that feels *too aligned to be accidental*, pause.
Your lineage is proud of you.

Sanjay Gandhi Post Graduate Institute of medical sciences (SGPGIMS), Lucknow

One morning in Kanpur, a chance encounter changed everything.
I met **Dr. Ashok Kumar Varshney** at the RSS office next to our home. Now he is the chief secretary of Aarogya Bharti (a non-profit organization). He completed his PhD in Biochemistry in 1986. He listened to my story and opened a door I hadn't even known existed.

SGPGIMS, Lucknow.

The same institute where my maternal grandfather had once been treated for liver cancer.
Life was circling back.
Dr. Varshney introduced to **Dr. M.M. Godbole**, a highly respected endocrinologist who would later receive the Padma Shri.

SGPGI was intimidating.
Forensic science did not exist there.
I was an outsider, academically and culturally.
I hope Dr. Godbole might take me on as a student. But he was close to retirement and needed someone who could contribute immediately. I was still learning the language of life sciences.
Yet, he did not shut the door.
Instead, he asked me to present a few topics in his lab seminars.
I studied. Prepared. Struggled.
During one presentation, he invited **Dr. K.N. Prasad from Microbiology department**, who would later become my PhD advisor.

As I stood there speaking on a topic completely new to me, something unexpected happened.
My voice was steady.
My delivery confident.
My fear... absent.

Dr. Godbole appreciated my presentation and personally recommended me to Dr. Prasad. Despite my lack of formal

training in life sciences, my sincerity and commitment were evident.
I was interviewed.

Then interviewed again by the Dean.
And through a series of alignments that still feel unreal, Dr. Godbole even offered to collaborate on my research.
That is how, in 2010, I began my PhD at SGPGIMS.

The Quiet Strength of Family

In the weeks leading up to my admission, I stayed with my cousins **Gudia and Shubham** in Lucknow. On the day of my PhD interview, my younger sister **Niharika** came with me.
My siblings: Niharika, Aishwarya, and Modak are not just my brothers and sisters.
They are my life witnesses.
My journal.
My shadow.
My quiet cheerleader.

Because I had left home early, for MSc, then PhD, I had limited time to build daily closeness with my siblings. Yet emotionally, I never left them. My bond with my sisters, Niharika and Vidhi, and brother, Modak, has always been deep, resilient, and anchored in unconditional emotional support for each other.

During my initial days at SGPGIMS with the new beginnings, I noticed a change within myself.

I was becoming a woman who could walk into rooms filled with people far more accomplished than herself, and still believe she deserved to be there.
I was no longer asking for permission.
I was **claiming my seat at the table**.

Reflection:

There will be moments in your life when you enter a room and feel like an imposter.
Too late.
Too underqualified.
Too different.
You'll wonder, *How did I even get here?*
But here is the truth: **if you reached that room, you earned your place in it**.
You may not yet speak the language fluently.
You may not know the rules or the hierarchy.
But your sincerity, preparation, and humility are universally understood.
When I entered SGPGIMS, I wasn't just changing institutions. I was changing disciplines. I did not have a master's in life sciences. No one there knew forensic science.

But I showed up anyway.
Not with arrogance.
Not with entitlement.
But with honesty and hunger to learn.
And that was enough.
Courage is often the only qualification you need to begin.
Divine timing matters, but it means nothing if you don't show up.

So even if you are uncertain.
Even if you feel invisible.
Even if you have no family legacy behind you,
Show up.
You may not be chosen every time.
But you will learn every time.
And one door, just one, will open.
That will be enough.
When it does, don't shrink.

Don't apologize for your journey.
Don't wish you were someone else.
Stand tall.
Breathe deeply.
And claim your seat at the table.

Message for Gen-Z Readers

This chapter is for you if you've ever thought:
"I did everything right... so why am I still confused?"
Clearing exams, getting degrees, collecting validations, none of them automatically give you clarity. Sometimes they only make the question louder: **What now?**

Here's the truth no one says out loud:
Feeling lost after a big win is normal.
Floating between options doesn't mean you failed, it means you're early.

I didn't have a clean plan.

I didn't neatly belong to one discipline.

I didn't even know if the next step would work.

What I had was **conviction before clarity**.

Dear fellows, you're growing up in a world obsessed with speed, certainty, and "figuring it out early." But real paths don't move in straight lines. They zigzag. They pause. They reroute.

Sometimes your next move won't come from logic, LinkedIn advice, or Google searches. It will come from a quiet inner knowing, the kind you feel before you can explain it.

If you're standing at a crossroads right now:

unsure

underqualified

out of place

Don't wait to feel ready.

Show up anyway.

Learn in public.

Let sincerity be your résumé.

You don't need to have the loudest voice in the room.

You just need the courage to sit at the table.

And when life gives you that seat, **take it**.

No shrinking.

No apologies.

No wishing you were someone else.

You belong more often than you think.

It is about what becomes possible when an average student is not arrested by fear and shows up.

Questions for the Reader:

- Where in your life are you waiting to feel "ready" before stepping forward?
- What part of you knows it's time to change direction, even if the path isn't clear yet?
- When you walk into unfamiliar spaces, do you shrink, or do you allow yourself to belong?
- What would it look like for you to claim your seat today, exactly as you are?

Presence Creates Legitimacy

Claiming My Seat at the Table

(PhD, New place, new struggles)

नायमात्मा बलहीनेन लभ्यः, Mundaka Upanishad 3.2.4

The self is not realized by the weak. Strength grows by staying when things are hard.

I didn't realize that my final journey from Delhi to Kanpur would change the way I viewed myself forever.
The day I left Delhi for Kanpur, with nothing but a bag and a brave heart, my friend handed me a fiction novel for the train ride, *2 States* by Chetan Bhagat. I had never read a novel before. I didn't even know how people read for pleasure. That night, somewhere between stations and silence, I finished the entire book in one sitting.

It was the story of two people falling in love in college from 2 different states, negotiating love, career, families, language, and belonging. At the time, it felt like a simple story, entertaining and light. I didn't know then that life was quietly offering me a preview.
Sometimes, books find you before the story begins.

A New World at SGPGIMS

Soon after, I got admission into SGPGIMS. I was trying to find my footing in a space that felt both intimidating and extraordinary. The institute did not feel like a college, it felt like a world unto itself. The corridors were quiet but heavy with purpose. Every face seemed serious, every conversation precise.

I remember walking into Dr. M. M. Godbole's lab for the first time. That was where I met a senior research scholar, Srikanth Garikipati, working under Dr. Sonia Nityanand, then she was the Head of Hematology and later the Vice Chancellor of KGMC, Lucknow. At that point, he was simply a senior research scholar, deeply focused, disciplined, and clearly respected in the lab.

Our paths crossed again and again, sometimes through science, sometimes through silence, sometime rushing over morning seminars, sometimes over those uncertain tea breaks where you don't know where your research is going, but the conversation makes you feel like you're not entirely lost alone.

Eventually, my time in Dr. Godbole's lab was reduced as I formally began working under my PhD advisor, Dr. K.N. Prasad. But the intellectual exchanges with Srikanth continued. What began as scientific brainstorming would, much later, become something more personal. At that time, though, I was far too consumed by survival to imagine anything else.

My PhD Topic: A Battle of Brain

My PhD thesis research was titled:
"Etiological characterization and immunopathogenesis of brain abscess."
My Advisor: Dr. Kashi Nath Prasad; Department of Microbiology, SGPGIMS
Co-advisor: Dr. B. K. Ojha; Head of the Department of Neurosurgery, KGMC
Co-advisor: Dr. Rakesh Gupta; Department of Radiology, SGPGIMS

Every single word in that sentence was foreign to me in the first 6 months of my PhD.

Immunology. Neurology. Microbiology. Radiology. I knew none of it. I came from forensic science, and suddenly I was expected to navigate complex disease mechanisms, immune pathways, and clinical realities of neurosurgery.
But I wasn't afraid.
Because by then, I had learned something important about myself: I pioneered the art of how to study new and hard things. And more importantly, I knew how to stay with them.

The first year of my PhD was brutal.
Every day, I spent hours reading, slowly, deliberately, often painfully. I wasn't skimming. I wasn't memorizing. I was trying to *understand*. Immunology does not reveal itself easily. Inflammation pathways, host immune responses, receptor cascades, nothing was intuitive. So, I made it personal.

I wrote my own notes. I made my own small drawings, rough sketches of cytokines communicating, arrows showing immune cells migrating, pathways drawn again and again until they finally made sense to me. Somewhere in that process, something shifted.
I learned **how to understand anything**.

That skill stayed with me for life.
But theory was only half the struggle.
Learning lab techniques was far harder.
Machines were finicky. Reagents were finicky. Protocols worked beautifully in books and failed miserably in real life. Sometimes, even people were finicky. In 2010, most of my experiments simply did not work. But every morning, I

returned to the lab and stood at the same bench again. I optimized. I failed. I tried again.
My learning had three sources: friends, seniors, and my own mistakes.
I stayed humble. I watched carefully. I asked questions. And when something finally worked, even a small success, I celebrated quietly. One coffee. One plate of Maggi. That was my reward.
Resilience, I learned, is not loud.
It is repetitive.
And it is built one failed experiment at a time.

Life on Neurosurgery Calls

Brain abscess sample from patients' collection meant frequent visits to King George Medical University (KGMC). My co-advisor, Dr. B. K. Ojha, was the Head of Neurosurgery there. Whenever a brain abscess case arrived, I was called, day or night.
I had to reach immediately.

I had full support from Dr. Ojha. I made friends among neurosurgeons and residents who supported me and helped me navigate that intense clinical environment. Still, the expectation was clear: availability was non-negotiable. And I met it, not for weeks, not for months, but for four continuous years.

The original idea of my PhD involved developing an animal model to study brain abscess. Srikanth and I would discuss experimental strategies to establish the animal models. Looking back now, those discussions were not just about research design. They were quietly teaching me how to think deeply, how to listen, how to persist.

Belonging, I learned, is not always about invitation.
Sometimes, it is about courage.
Readiness comes *after* the leap.

The scientific Stage Called

After thousands of hours of reading, failing, refining, and trying again, my experiments began to yield reliable data. I wrote and submitted my first abstract to IAMM 2011 at Banaras Hindu University.
It was accepted for oral presentation.

The stage was calling me again. But this time, not to perform, but *to present*. To stand not as a student unsure of her place, but as a researcher sharing her research.
Then life intervened.

I discovered a big lump in my chest. Medical attention followed quickly. Lab tests confirmed it was a fibroadenoma, benign, but large enough to require surgical removal. I still feel surprised about how casual it remained for me to go for mammograms, MRI and biopsy in between my experiments and return to lab like nothing happened. All lab tests by myself. Mission PhD was so huge and important to me that even my health became small before it.
The surgery was scheduled.
But I made a decision.

I told my surgeon, "Let me do my oral presentation first. Then I'll come back for surgery."
He agreed.
At Banaras Hindu University, my research was appreciated. I met peers, professors, and mentors. I answered questions confidently. I felt, perhaps for the first time, that I belonged.
When I returned, I had surgery.

I remember the pre-surgery room clearly, it was full of my friends. My mother was there too. Even at that moment, the atmosphere was unexpectedly light. There were laughter and casual banter, as if we were not about to go through a serious medical procedure but simply sharing another ordinary moment. Perhaps that was how each of us managed our fear.

Then I was taken into the operating room. The doctor administered general anesthesia. Before the medication took effect, surgeon began asking me questions about my own research. I kept answering, talking about my research, my thesis, my experiments. And somewhere in the middle of explaining my research, I slipped into the effects of anesthesia. I don't remember the moment I lost consciousness.

When I woke up, the surgery was already over. I was in the post-surgery room. As I became aware of my surroundings, I saw a few of my friends there, waiting to see me. In that moment, there was no fear or heaviness, only a quiet sense that everything had gone fine, and that I was not alone.
Recovery took a few weeks. And then I went back to the lab again.

Reflection:

That year, 2011, taught me more than any textbook ever could.
It taught me to trust myself. To listen to my body. To respect timing. To believe in second chances.

I was no longer the "average student" who didn't know how to score in class. By the time I reached SGPGIMS, I had already become an academic topper. I qualified for national level UGC-JRF. On paper, I was accomplished.
But inside, I was still learning to claim my seat at the table.

And I did, slowly, imperfectly, honestly.
To every student reading this: your first topic, your first year, your first failure may feel overwhelming. But mountains become climbable when you take one committed step at a time.
Sometimes, what looks like a detour, a book on a train, a health scare, a conversation over tea, is actually part of your design.
Even the universe pauses to admire those who don't give up.

That year, 2011, taught me lessons no textbook could. It taught me that growth is rarely synchronized. Achievement can outpace belief. Titles can arrive before identity. The world may recognize you before you recognize yourself.

I did not stop being that middle-class girl. But slowly, I began to understand that my fear was no longer needed to write my introductions. My past could explain me, but it no longer had the authority to define me.

There is a quiet trap that waits for new achievers, especially those from modest beginnings, the temptation to hold on to the old identity because it feels familiar, safe, and morally correct. Staying small can masquerade as humility. Self-effacement can feel like loyalty to where you came from. But over time, this attachment becomes a ceiling.

Carrying the old identity for too long does not keep you grounded; it keeps you stalled. The world does not reward unclaimed growth. If you hesitate to own your achievements, others will decide their value for you, and often, they will decide you are optional. Not because you lack merit, but because you never claimed your seat.

I learned that embracing achievement is not arrogance; it is responsibility. When you do not name your work, when you soften your presence, when you wait to be invited repeatedly, you leave space for the world to sideline you quietly. Progress does not protect you from erasure, clarity does.

There is another truth I came to understand slowly: you do not need to fight the world to justify your place. You do not need to argue, explain, or defend why you belong at the table. Constant explanation drains energy and quietly shifts the burden of proof back onto you.

Belonging, at this stage, is an act of perseverance rather than persuasion. You claim your seat by staying seated. By returning again and again. By continuing to contribute, to speak with specificity, to do the work visibly and consistently. Over time, presence itself becomes proof.

To move forward, I had to do something deeply uncomfortable: acknowledge that I belonged and remain there without apology. Let others adjust. Let discomfort exist. The old identity had served its purpose, but it could not be allowed to lead anymore. Growth demands not just effort, but ownership, and the quiet perseverance to keep showing up at the table once you have claimed it.

Questions for the Reader:

- What hard thing are you avoiding because it feels overwhelming?
- How do you respond when progress is slow?
- Are you willing to give time and attention to something before it gives results?
- Where are you still mistaking comfort for humility?
- What part of your old identity is quietly limiting you?
- What would it look like to claim your seat before the world decides it for you?

Cross Your Horizon

Stepping into the Unknown

(First flight to USA)

अभ्यासेन तु कौन्तेय वैराग्येण च गृह्यते- Bhagavad Gita 6.35

You don't level up by motivation. You level up by showing up.

Again. And again. And again.

Returning from Banaras Hindu University, I felt renewed, lighter in my body after the surgery, and steadier in my mind after standing on stage and speaking for my research. Presenting my research in front of peers, professors, and senior scientists gave me a quiet but powerful adrenaline rush. It wasn't loud confidence. It was something deeper, a sense that I could *hold my ground*.

I carried that feeling straight back into the lab.
Life at SGPGIMS resumed its rhythm, or more accurately, its relentless pulse. By then, I had learned that research life does not unfold in chapters. It moves in cycles, often repetitive, often exhausting, and rarely glamorous.
My days looked like this:
Urgent calls from KGMC for brain abscess sample collection, sometimes at odd hours.
Long hours of experiments that refused to work the way textbooks promised.

8 a.m. morning seminars that demanded full attention even after sleepless nights.
Stacks of research papers marked with underlines, arrows, and handwritten questions.
Protocols written, rewritten, optimized, and discarded.
Late-night experiments followed by early-morning returns to the same bench.

Everything revolved around the PhD.
It consumed me, not in a dramatic way, but in a slow, complete way. My calendar, my body clock, my thoughts, and even my dreams were shaped by experiments, results, and unanswered questions.

SGPGIMS was no ordinary place. It was a high-pressure academic ecosystem where excellence was the baseline, not the exception. Walking through those pristine corridors meant passing Padma Shri awardees, Bhatnagar Laureates, and pioneers whose work had changed the landscape of Indian medicine and science. The environment was both inspiring and intimidating.

Everywhere I looked, people were doing *real* work, research that mattered. Scholars were publishing in top journals, receiving national recognition, and securing prestigious postdoctoral positions abroad.
Some days, the contrast felt overwhelming.
But SGPGIMS was not just about research. It was about life unfolding alongside science. The corridors were filled with patients and families waiting with quiet hope. Doctors moved swiftly between surgeries. Students balanced academic pressure with clinical realities. I often watched surgeons sitting silently with a cup of tea late at night, just after finishing an exhausting operation, while I ran my experiments two labs away.
That sight taught me something no lecture ever could:
There is no substitute for hard work when lives are at stake.

Learning to Endure

Even amid that intensity, we all, as research scholars, found ways to breathe.
There were informal dinners at Aryan, Motimahal, and Royal Café in Lucknow, farewells for seniors, celebrations for accepted papers, reunions with alumni who returned briefly

before leaving again for the world beyond. Sometimes, when time did not permit, celebrations happened right by the lab, cake placed carefully beside reagent boxes, laughter bouncing off centrifuges, someone clicking photos while another watched the timer.

The lab was not just a workspace. It was home.
And the people in it, fellow scholars, technicians, seniors, juniors, became a second family. We learned to depend on each other not just for protocols, but for reassurance. For those moments when nothing worked and quitting felt tempting.
By this point, I knew one thing clearly: talent might open doors, but *stamina* decides who stays.

A Turning Point in 2012

Then came a moment that quietly shifted my inner horizon.
In 2012, I submitted my research abstract to the Society for Neuroscience (SFN), one of the largest and most prestigious neuroscience conferences in the world, held that year in New Orleans, Louisiana.
When the acceptance email arrived, I read it twice. Then a third time.

My abstract had been accepted for a poster presentation.
Excitement was followed almost immediately by reality.
Acceptance was only the first hurdle.
To even become a member of SFN, I needed recommendations from established scientists. I didn't know many. Still, I wrote emails, carefully, respectfully, and

without expectation, to researchers across India, explaining my work and requesting support.
Most did not reply.

But two kind souls did. They endorsed my application. I still remember that generosity. At that stage of life, even small acts of belief feel monumental.
Then came funding.

My fellowship had only just begun. Whatever savings I had, they largely went toward supporting my family. Self-sponsoring an international trip was not an option.
But giving up was never part of my vocabulary.

I applied to the Department of Biotechnology for a travel grant. They reviewed my academic record and partially funded my journey. For the remaining amount, I borrowed money from close friends, people who trusted my intentions and believed in my dream.

And just like that, through a mixture of effort, faith, and collective support, I was preparing to fly to the United States.
Alone, all by myself.
For the first time.

Not just for myself, but for every girl from a small town who dares to dream beyond what she has seen.
I was still that same girl who once didn't know how to score 60% in class.

The same "average" student.

And now, I was going to the USA to present my research on a global platform, funded by the Government of India.
During my childhood, my Nana would always point to the airplanes every single time our bus crossed the Lucknow airport.

And today, from that very same airport, I boarded a flight to the United States.
What was once lived only as a distant dream became real that day, carried by the blessings, hopes, and quiet faith of many souls who had shaped my life.
That realization sat heavy and beautiful in my chest.

Crossing the Horizon and continents

Flying to the United States changed something fundamental inside me.
My route was New Delhi → Chicago → New Orleans. When I stepped out of the airport at Chicago, it felt like landing on another planet. Everything looked different. Sounded different. Moved differently.

There, I met a familiar face, Amrita Pathak, an SGPGIMS alumna and one of my seniors, then doing her postdoc at Vanderbilt University. She introduced me to her advisor and colleagues, bridging my fear with familiarity.
That conference became a portal.

I met faculty members, postdocs, and students from Nobel laureate labs. I listened to conversations that stretched my imagination of what science could be. The scale, the ambition, the confidence, it all felt overwhelming and exhilarating at once.

Being vegetarian in the U.S. required creativity. For most days, my meals consisted of burger buns with salad or French fries. I quickly learned that ordering a regular coffee was easier than navigating endless choices. For seven days, my diet was predictable: bread with salad, regular coffee, Coke, and water.

When I finally saw naan, dal makhani, and rice at the conference one evening, it felt like a warm hug to my soul.
American conferences were different. Nothing was free, no food, no kits, no hospitality. Everything was paid for. It was a culture shock, but also a lesson in independence.
At that time, only a handful of labs worldwide were working on brain abscess. One of them was led by Tammy Kielian. I met her too.

Standing there, listening, observing, absorbing, I had a quiet thought:
Look at how far you've come, Anamika. And at the same time amazed by the science!

Reflection:

That trip was not just a milestone, it was a mirror.
I was no longer questioning whether I belonged in science. I was questioning how far I was willing to go.
I often wonder what my parents felt watching me leave for the USA for the first time. I won't reopen everything I was

carrying personally at that moment. But I will say this: I was proud.

Not as a scientist.
Not as an adult.
But as that girl from 9th grade who was once average, confused, and failed academically.
This was her victory.
And it was never mine alone.
It was a cumulative act of blessings, mentors, friends, strangers, institutions, and moments of grace aligning quietly. I was only a medium, to present research, to represent my institute, my advisor, my department, my country, and the name I carry.
That is both humbling and empowering.
I never resonated with the phrase *"believe in yourself and the world will believe in you."* What carried me instead was something simpler and more stubborn:

This can't be it.
Life can't be this small.
It has to grow.
Because everything divine grows.
And if you are growing, even slowly, you are aligned.

A Message to the Average Student

To every student who believes they are ordinary, unsure, or behind,
Let me tell you something I learned slowly, through years of effort, failure, and faith:

You already carry everything you need to become who you want to be.
Nothing essential is missing.
When I was younger, between Grade 9 and my first year of BSc, my self-esteem was very low. I did not know how to score well in exam. I did not feel intelligent or exceptional. I had quietly accepted a narrow future shaped by family expectations, environment, and financial realities.

I believed my life would unfold within those boundaries.
That belief was my only real limitation.
Tat Tvam Asi means **"You are that."**
It means the potential you admire, the life you imagine, the excellence you see in others, it already exists within you. Not magically, not effortlessly, but **latently**. Waiting.
Do not arrest yourself with the invisible cuffs of your surroundings.
Do not shrink your dreams to match your finances, your neighborhood, or what people around you believe is "realistic."
Once you decide what you want to become, truly decide, the universe begins to rearrange itself around that intention.
I did not have a blueprint.
I did not have connections.
I did not even have confidence.
What I had was one quiet decision: *I will walk toward something meaningful.*
For me, that "something" was science.
For you, it could be art, law, literature, social work, entrepreneurship, teaching, anything that makes you feel alive.
But hear this clearly:
Do not choose your life based only on money.
Do not chase what looks easy or immediately

rewarding. A life built without inner conviction does not sustain you for forty years.
If you are around 23 years old, this is the most important question you can ask yourself:
Can I fall in love with this work enough to do it for the next decade?
Because only love, for the work itself, will carry you through failures, boredom, slow progress, and uncertainty.
You do not need all the logistics.
You do not need permission.
You do not need certainty.
You only need to imagine, honestly and courageously, where you want to go.
Think.
Choose.
Walk.
Let the universe take care of the path.
Because when intention is clear, and effort is sincere, **everything finds its way.**
Tat tvam Asi.
You are that. You don't need to find it anywhere outside!!

Questions for the Reader:

- What does "staying" mean for you right now?
- Are you mistaking slow progress for failure?
- What comfort zone is asking to be stretched?
- What part of you is ready for the next horizon even if you're afraid?

Integrity Sustains Growth

Rising to the Moment

(Choosing love, cruising through PhD)

तमेव भान्तमनुभाति सर्वं , Mundaka Upanishad 2.2.10

When That shines, everything shines after it. By its light, all of this is illuminated.

Returning to India after my first trip to the United States felt less like coming back and more like arriving as someone new. I wasn't the same girl who had left for the conference just weeks earlier. Something inside me had shifted, not loudly, not dramatically, but permanently.

I was sharper. More grounded. And for the first time, I carried a quiet confidence that did not come from approval, but from exposure. I had seen what world-class science looked like. I had stood among global researchers. And somewhere in that experience, a subtle realization settled in:
I belonged there, too.
Back in India, I had another oral presentation lined up, **IAMM 2012**.

This time, my confidence was rocket high.
The nervousness that once sat heavy in my chest was gone. Having witnessed cutting-edge science, interacted with scientists trained in Nobel laureate labs, and observed how questions were asked and answered on international platforms, my internal benchmark had changed. I walked into IAMM with a different posture, physically and mentally.
I could hear it in my voice.
I could feel it in my body language.
I could see it in how I responded to questions.

My presentation went flawlessly, not because it was perfect, but because I was no longer trying to prove myself. I had already accepted myself.

Over the next two years, **2013 and 2014**, my research momentum accelerated. I presented multiple posters at national conferences. I gave oral presentations. I engaged more deeply with my work, not anxiously, but deliberately. That same period marked several milestones I had once believed were reserved for "other people."

My **first-author international publications** were accepted.
And co-authored manuscripts followed.
I received an **international travel grant from the Government of India**.
I began writing my **PhD thesis**.

And quietly, without announcement, I started applying for **postdoctoral positions in the United States**.
And just like that, the girl who once wondered if she belonged,
Was now writing scientific conclusions.
Was now preparing to fly again.
Was now a scientist.
There was no grand plan behind it. No blueprint. No five-year chart pinned to a wall.
Some things in life are not planned.
They are written.

But they only reveal themselves when you start walking, even if all you have is a backpack, a notebook, and belief.
Sometimes, we think we are just attending a seminar...
But we are actually walking into destiny.
Sometimes, we think we're sending an email to a travel grant...

But we're unlocking doors we cannot yet see.

What happened to me was not luck.
It was alignment.
The cumulative blessing of everyone who stood beside me:
My family.
My mentors.
My seniors.
My lab.
My institute.

I was only the medium, the one standing on stage, presenting work that carried more than just my name. It carried my family's name, my mentor's words, my institute's trust, and the quiet resilience of a girl who had once doubted herself.

And this is what I learned during that phase:
When the intention is pure and the goal is larger than the self, the universe becomes your lab partner.
When I look back now, it still amazes me.
No one in my family had imagined I would go to SGPGIMS.
No one thought I would pursue a PhD.
I had never dreamed of becoming a scientist, let alone marrying one.
I became the **first PhD scholar in my family**.

The **first scientist**.
The **first girl who chose her own life partner**.
The **first girl to go abroad**.
And I did all of this not by knowing what would come next, but by being willing to show up fully where I was.

Srikanth: Choosing Love After Becoming Myself

Srikanth (now my husband) entered my life quietly.
There was no dramatic beginning.
No romantic declaration.
No promise of comfort, wealth, or certainty.

We were both research scholars, living on fellowships, managing modest lives. We didn't have much money. We didn't have elaborate plans. In fact, if someone had asked me then whether this was "love," I wouldn't have known what to say.

I didn't even know what to call it.
What I did know was this:
I didn't see a reason to walk away.
By then, SGPGIMS had already reshaped me. I was no longer looking to be rescued or completed. I was learning how to stand firmly in who I was becoming.
Srikanth did not interrupt that process.
He did not rush it.
He did not diminish it.
What made me stayed with him was not affection or pampering, it was **steadiness**.

I observed how he treated people.
How he spoke to juniors.
How he handled pressure.
How he listened without needing to fix.
There was consistency. Integrity. Quiet discipline.

In my generation, marriage was something most girls did by default. But I knew I could not enter it blindly. What made my decision clear was this simple truth:
Being with him did not shrink me.
I did not need to perform.
I did not need to explain my ambition.
I did not need to become smaller to feel safe.
There were no guarantees, only shared values and emotional clarity.
I did not choose certainty.
I chose integrity.
And that choice has endured.

We both got married in 2014 in the presence of friends and both sides of the families under the shower of lots of love and blessings. When I entered Srikanth's family, I carried the visible markers of difference — language, region, upbringing. Yet, from the very beginning, I was embraced as a daughter. The North–South divide that so often defines identity in India, but their love was larger than culture, stronger than language, and gentler than any hesitation I had carried. In that acceptance, I learned that belonging is not created by similarity, but by generosity of heart.

A Message to Young Women: Choosing a Life Partner Without Hurry

Love does not need urgency.
Life does not reward haste.
If you are young and feeling pressured to decide quickly, pause.

Do not choose someone because of attention, pampering, or fear of being left behind. Instead, observe how a person treats the world around them. Notice their actions when things are difficult. Watch how they handle silence, frustration, and responsibility.
Slow reveals what fast hides.

Choose from clarity, not fear.
Choose someone who walks beside you, not ahead of you, not over you.
A relationship is not meant to rescue you from life.
It is meant to walk with you as you grow.

Reflection:

By the first half of 2014, I could finally see the finish line. My thesis was taking shape. My research was solid. And I was preparing quietly for the next unknown.
I had once arrived at SGPGIMS unsure of myself.
I was leaving as a scholar, a partner, and a woman transformed.
What this phase taught me is simple but enduring:
You do not need a full map to move forward.
You need honesty, effort, and faith.
If your path feels unclear, it does not mean you are lost. It may mean you are growing beyond old definitions.
You are allowed to walk without knowing where every step leads.
That, too, is courage.

Questions for the Reader:

- Where in your life are you waiting for certainty before taking action?
- Who are you becoming even if no one else has noticed yet?
- What would change if you trusted your effort more than outcomes?
- Who walks beside you without diminishing your growth?

Finish Before Flight

The Work Before the Flight to Unknown

(PhD, wedding bells, new life)

कुर्वन्नेवेह कर्माणि जिजीविषेत् शतं समाः — Isha Upanishad 2
Real progress is built through consistent work long before the outcome becomes visible.

The months before leaving India were not dramatic. They were dense.
They were filled with work that did not look heroic from the outside but demanded everything from the inside. This was the phase where nothing was celebrated yet, no farewell, no flight, no visible arrival. It was simply the work before the flight.

During the Late 2013 and first half of 2014, my days revolved around finishing what I had started. I was submitting scientific manuscripts to journals, formatting them exactly as per journal guidelines, revising and rerevising them multiple times, responding to reviewers, facing rejections, and resubmitting. In science, rejection is not an exception, it is the default. Experiments fail. Hypotheses collapse. Reagents don't work. Scientific articles are rejected. Grants don't get funded. Applications disappear into silence.
As scientists, we learn early that failure is not personal, it is procedural. We fail daily, sometimes hourly. And yet, we return to the question.

That is the core of research life: living with unanswered questions and still showing up the next day to search for answers. Sometimes solutions arrive during seminars. Sometimes during chai breaks. Sometimes, while walking through corridors. Sometimes in casual conversations with friends. Any moment can trigger insight, because research is not confined to the lab, it occupies the mind constantly.
By then, I was also writing my PhD thesis.

At the same time, I began applying for postdoctoral fellowship positions in the United States. What followed was a long stretch of persistence that tested my patience more than my intelligence. Nearly a hundred application emails. Close to a dozen interviews. Long periods of waiting. Follow-ups that went unanswered. Promising conversations that led nowhere.

This phase required quiet endurance.
Between April and December 2014, life became intensely busy. I was juggling final experiments, data compilation, thesis writing, manuscript revisions, and living in Lucknow, while frequently traveling to Kanpur and Hyderabad, moving between my parents' home and my in-laws. The pace was physically exhausting and emotionally demanding.

Marriage brought its own adjustments. In India, the first year after marriage carries many rituals, expectations, and social responsibilities. As a newly married woman, I tried to honor those traditions while still holding on to my academic commitments. It was not easy. There were days when the boundaries between personal life and professional life disappeared entirely.

During this time, my PhD advisor became a pillar of support. His understanding, flexibility, and trust allowed me to complete my research without feeling diminished for choosing both family and ambition. That balance mattered more than I understood at the time.

Eventually, after months of effort and uncertainty, I received an offer for a postdoctoral fellowship in Biomedical Engineering at Drexel University.
Relief came quietly, not as a celebration, but as steadiness.

By December 2014, I submitted my thesis. The end of the PhD was not marked by fireworks or grand emotion. It felt more like releasing a breath that I had been holding for years. The work was complete.

But one more challenge remained.
The J-1 Research Scholar visa process.
It required extensive documentation, repeated communication between Drexel University and the U.S. Embassy, and weeks of waiting without certainty. Every email notification triggered hope. Every delay tested patience. Eventually, the visa came through.

Before leaving India, I spent a month in Kanpur, and then returned once more to Hyderabad. There, I packed two suitcases containing the essence of my twenty-seven years of life, clothes, Indian utensils, homemade pickles, memories, faith, and God's blessings.

It was the day after Makar Sankranti when I boarded my flight from Hyderabad to New York.
What I remember most clearly is this: there was no fear.
I felt calm. Neutral. Grounded.
Srikanth was already in Philadelphia. I was stepping into the next phase of my life, not rushed, not dramatic, but ready.
This chapter of my life did not end with applause. It ended with quiet completion.
And that quiet readiness carried me forwardacross an ocean, into a world I was about to learn from the beginning.

Reflection:

Looking back, this phase taught me something essential: progress often happens long before visibility.
The months before leaving India were not glamorous. They were repetitive, exhausting, and full of uncertainty. But they built a kind of strength that cannot be rushed, a strength that comes from finishing what you start, even when outcomes are unclear.

Rejections did not mean I was failing. They meant I was participating.
Every unanswered email, every rejected manuscript, every delayed interview trained me to separate self-worth from external validation. That lesson would later become crucial during immigration, motherhood, career pauses, and reinvention.

This period also taught me that life rarely offers clean transitions. You often close one chapter while emotionally still inside it. You grieve familiarity while preparing for change. You carry responsibility while dreaming of freedom.
For students, researchers, and young professionals reading this: understand that preparation is not always visible. Sometimes, the most important work happens in silence, while no one is watching.

If you are currently in a phase filled with rejection, waiting, or uncertainty, know this: you are not behind. You are building endurance.
The work you do before your “flight, literal or metaphorical, will decide how you land.

Questions for the Reader:

- What unfinished work in your life needs patience rather than urgency?
- How do you respond to rejection, do you retreat, or do you return to the question?
- Are you confusing visibility with readiness?
- What kind of strength are you building right now that no one can see yet?
- If your next chapter required quiet preparation, would you be willing to stay with the process?

Adapt. Anchor. Advance.

Postdoctoral Life: Learning to Live Between Worlds

(Two Suitcases, Two Postdocs, and a Foreign Winter)

विद्या विनयेन शोभते।, *Taittiriya Upanishad 1.11*

Knowledge shines only when paired with humility.

I landed at JFK Airport in New York in January 2015, into sub-normal freezing temperatures that felt both physical and symbolic. The cold cut through my jacket, my confidence, and everything familiar. I had crossed an ocean, a time zone, and a lifetime of assumptions in a single flight.
Within a week of landing, I joined Drexel University as a postdoctoral fellow in the Department of Biomedical Engineering.

At that time, Srikanth was already in Philadelphia, working as a postdoctoral fellow at Temple University. He had rented a small studio apartment in University City, Philadelphia. That modest space, compact, functional, and shared, quietly became the beginning of our married life and our life in the United States.
There was nothing grand about that beginning. No spacious home. No elaborate plans. No glossy, fancy life. Just a handful of things. Two postdocs, two suitcases, and a shared determination to build a life anchored in work, values, and patience.

I joined Dr. Kara Spiller's lab in department of biomedical engineering at Drexel University. My lab at Drexel was about a mile from our apartment. Some days I walked; other days I took the tram. Very often, Srikanth would walk from Temple to Drexel so that we could return home together. On those walks back, we almost always shared a single cup of coffee with some French fries. It was a small ritual, one cup, two people, but it grounded us. Even though we were married and officially "postdocs," our lives still felt remarkably similar to our PhD days: tight schedules, limited resources, and total immersion in science. Research life is never rich money-wise but it is highly rich intellectually.

A postdoc, I soon realized, is essentially an extension of a PhD, designing experiments, performing them, analyzing data, publishing papers, and attending lab meetings. In postdoctoral training, soft skills become as important as technical expertise. A postdoc is no longer just executing experiments; they are expected to think independently, manage projects, collaborate across disciplines, mentor students, communicate findings clearly, and often navigate multicultural research environments. The ability to articulate ideas in meetings, write persuasive grants and manuscripts, resolve conflicts within teams, manage time across competing priorities, and build professional networks directly influences visibility and career progression. Many brilliant researchers plateau not because of a lack of intelligence, but because they struggle with communication, leadership, or strategic relationship-building. Strong soft skills transform a postdoc from a technically competent researcher into a future principal investigator, industry leader, or entrepreneurial scientist capable of shaping both science and people. The difference was not the work itself, but the world in which it was happening.
This was no longer India.
This was the United States.
Professionally, I was a postdoctoral fellow.

Personally, I was learning how to live between worlds.
Everything felt unfamiliar at first, almost disorienting. The roads were wider. The signboards looked different. Buildings

were taller, more uniform, and quieter. Faces were unfamiliar. Even the sky looked different, less crowded, less noisy, more still. Time itself felt altered. I was suddenly living by EST instead of IST. While my family in India was waking up, my day was ending. Festivals, birthdays, casual conversations, everything now required planning, calculation, and intention.

Even the language I spoke daily felt subtly foreign. I had grown up with Indian English, shaped by British grammar, academic formality, and shared cultural references. American English was faster, more casual, more conversational. The words were familiar, but the rhythm was different. I had to learn not just what to say, but how to say it, without losing myself.

Beyond geography and language, the academic culture was profoundly different.
In India, my education had been shaped by the guru–shishya tradition, formal or informal, but deeply ingrained. Professors were mentors, guides, and authority figures. Juniors observed seniors closely, learned by watching, and built bonds through shared struggle. Respect was cultural, not negotiated.

In the United States, academic relationships are flatter. First names replaced titles. Hierarchies were subtle or invisible. While this encouraged independence and confidence, it also lacked something I had unconsciously relied on, the warmth of structured mentorship, the quiet protection that seniors sometimes offered in Indian academic spaces. Junior–

senior bonding was limited. Everyone was professional, efficient, and self-directed, but often alone.
This difference is not good or bad.
It was simply different.
And learning to function without familiar scaffolding required emotional adjustment.
Daily life demanded its own education.

Ordering coffee was not instinctive. I had to learn what "regular," "decaf," "cream," and "half-and-half" meant, and why a simple request led to a cascade of questions. Ordering a sandwich required patience and repetition, confirming again and again that it did not contain meat, explaining vegetarian preferences, and learning new food vocabulary that had never existed in my Indian life. At restaurants, I often repeated myself three or four times just to be certain.
Even crossing the road felt unfamiliar. Pedestrian signals counted down loudly, twenty seconds to cross, no hesitation allowed. I learned to walk faster, think quicker, and trust unfamiliar systems.

These moments may seem trivial, but together they reshaped my confidence. Slowly, daily survival turned into daily competence. And daily competence turned into quiet belonging.
At the same time, I was learning how to be a wife in a completely new setting.

Srikanth is deeply social, and our apartment was rarely quiet. Friends, visiting scholars, and acquaintances flowed in and out. Monday through Friday, we lived as scientists. Weekends were devoted to hospitality, cooking, hosting, walking through the city, and building friendships. This rhythm was different from my life in India, but slowly, it became our own.

In India, I had lived in hostels. Life was communal. Meals were mostly prepared for us. Support systems were built into daily life. I had never balanced intensive research with household responsibilities at the same time. In the United States, everything had to be done independently. There were no mess halls, no domestic help, no extended family nearby. Learning to manage a home, a marriage, and a demanding research schedule simultaneously required maturity I did not know I possessed.

At the same time, I was adapting to a new research culture. My lab had fourteen members, all American. My advisor was American. I was the only Indian in the group. In the entire department, there were very few Indian postdoctoral fellows.

Initially, understanding accents and informal communication took effort. Meetings moved fast. Jokes were cultural. References were local. Fitting in did not come naturally, but withdrawal was not an option. Slowly, I learned to speak up, to ask questions, to laugh even when I didn't fully understand the humor. I learned how to belong without trying to imitate.

Science became my bridge.

At SGPGIMS, I learned the foundations of collaboration. At Drexel, that learning expanded dramatically. My projects now span four universities, including the University of Pennsylvania, six departments, and teams of nearly twenty

people. Collaboration was constant and structured. Much of it happened through long threads, careful wording, and clarity of intent in emails. I learned that communication was not a soft skill; it was a scientific necessity.
During this time, I mentored two master's students. Teaching clarified my own thinking. I also witnessed, up close, a dynamic woman principal investigator, leading with authority, confidence, and intellectual depth. Watching her quietly expanded my imagination of what leadership could look like.

Late evenings in the lab became routine. At home, hospitality remained constant. I learned how to host the guests and still return to the lab the same day. This phase demanded endurance, physical and emotional.
I published several high-impact papers. The work mattered. It anchored me when everything else felt unfamiliar.

Yet beneath the surface lived a quiet homesickness. I missed my family. I missed my friends. I missed being known without explanation. This missing did not announce itself. It lived quietly alongside gratitude. Personally, it confirmed something deeper: living between worlds does not dilute identity, it refines it. During my time at Drexel, I worked relentlessly, days and nights blurred into experiments, data, and deadlines. The laboratory became my primary world, and alongside my research, I was learning how to live in the United States independently, deliberately, and far from familiarity.

I published impactful scientific findings and grew technically stronger with each project. On paper, it was a productive and successful phase.
And yet, beneath that progress, there was an absence I could not ignore.
I did not have a true mentor during this time, someone who could guide not just the science, but the scientist.
After three years, I moved to Temple University School of Medicine, Center for Translational Medicine. Professionally, it marked growth.

Reflection:

Living between worlds teaches you lessons no syllabus ever will.
As a postdoctoral fellow in the United States, I was not just learning science. I was learning how to exist without familiar anchors. The lab taught me experimental rigor, but life outside it taught me emotional discipline. In India, belonging had been automatic. In the U.S., it had to be built slowly, deliberately, sometimes painfully.

This phase of my life revealed how much of our confidence is contextual. In Indian academic spaces, I knew where I stood. Hierarchies, expectations, and relationships, however imperfect, were familiar. In the U.S., merit was individual, independence was assumed, and support systems were quieter. You were expected to advocate for yourself, design your own boundaries, and carry your ambitions without visible reassurance.
For many PhD students and postdocs, especially immigrants, this transition is not merely professional. It is

deeply personal. You are asked to perform at your best while translating yourself constantly: your language, your humor, your silence, your values. You learn quickly that intelligence alone is not enough. Adaptability, humility, and patience become survival skills.

At the same time, you discover the strength you did not know you had.
Balancing research with marriage, hospitality, cultural adjustments, and quiet homesickness taught me that growth is rarely comfortable. Some days, progress felt invisible. Some evenings, exhaustion came not from experiments, but from emotional translation, deciding when to explain, when to adjust, and when to simply remain yourself.

Yet, this phase mattered.
It prepared me for everything that came next, the demands of motherhood, the grief of loss, the courage required to pause, and eventually, the strength to return. Living between worlds stretched me without breaking me. It taught me how to stand alone without becoming isolated, how to belong without disappearing, and how to keep moving even when certainty was unavailable.

For those still walking this path, know this: feeling unsettled does not mean you are failing. It often means you are growing. Learning to live between worlds is not about choosing one over the other. It is about carrying both with integrity.
And that ability, to hold complexity without losing yourself, will become your greatest asset.

Questions for the Reader:

- In what ways are you currently living between worlds culturally, professionally, or emotionally?
- What parts of your identity feel stretched, and which feel strengthened?
- How do you cope with invisibility, homesickness, or lack of familiar support systems?
- What skills are you developing outside the lab that may matter just as much as your research?
- If this phase prepares you for something ahead, what might it be shaping in you?

Pause Without Surrender

Molecules, Motherhood, and the Cost of Continuity

(Between Laboratory Timelines and Lullabies and Pandemic)

यस्यामतं तस्य मतं, मतं यस्य न वेद सः
अविज्ञातं विजानतां, विज्ञातमविजानताम् — **Kena Upanishad, 2.3**

Those who think they fully understand the truth do not truly know it. Those who realize that it cannot be fully known are the ones who begin to understand.

I joined the Lewis Katz School of Medicine at Temple University in Philadelphia, USA, in 2018 as a postdoctoral fellow. My principal investigator, Dr. Douglas Tilley, was trained with a Nobel laureate team. The department chair, Dr. Walter Koch, had also trained under a Nobel laureate. I also met 2012 Nobel laureate Brian Kobalika in one of our seminars, as we both shared GPCRs research legacy. The department itself was built and sustained by scientists whose work had shaped cardiovascular medicine over decades.

These were not simply accomplished researchers. These were people whose names appeared repeatedly in textbooks, whose discoveries informed clinical guidelines, whose work quietly influenced how heart-attack patients were treated across the world. To be surrounded by such minds every day was both intimidating and deeply energizing.
I was working with pioneers.

My research focused on beta-blocker drugs, medications already prescribed to heart-attack patients as standard care. Yet despite their widespread use, clinical outcomes were inconsistent. Some patients responded exceptionally well. Others showed limited benefits. Some improved initially and then declined. My question was direct, almost unsettling in its simplicity:

Why does the same drug work for some patients and not for others?
That single question opened an entire universe. It pulled me into molecular signaling pathways, immune modulation,

receptor sensitivity, and patient-specific disease mechanisms. I wasn't looking for quick answers. I was learning how much complexity hides beneath what medicine often calls "standard treatment."

This was the science I loved, science that respected uncertainty, that asked better questions instead of offering comfortable conclusions. Now I have been exploring thc role of one kind of immune cells, macrophage cells, in several sterile and non-sterile inflammation in the human body. Now I humbly accept that I knew a lot of macrophages that I didn't know in 2010. My expertise with these cells had expanded to the level that I could think about these cells in a much better way than others.

My days were dense. Weekly research seminars introduced me to cutting-edge work in cardiovascular biology and immunology. I learned how to develop heart-attack models in mice, how to perform bone-marrow transplantation, how to execute precise injections, how to run echocardiography, and how to analyze flow-cytometry data that rarely behaved neatly. I learned how to write grants, not just technically, but strategically.

Some experiments ran for fifteen hours straight. Many nights, I stayed in the lab until 3 a.m., running between buildings, hopping from lab to lab, waiting for time points, checking controls, and troubleshooting protocols that refused to cooperate. I remember walking through empty hallways at night, the hum of equipment my only company, feeling both exhausted and alive.

I was tired, but I was happy.
Work has always made me happy, but only when it is meaningful. I need intellectual honesty, creative freedom, and room to decide. At Temple University, I had all of that. I was trusted. I was challenged. I was learning fast.

Around me, postdoctoral fellows were winning grants and transitioning into faculty positions across the United States. Their success didn't intimidate me. It filled my eyes with sparks. It reminded me that growth was possible, that effort mattered, that paths were opening.

By the time I joined Temple University, six years had passed since my marriage. Life had moved quickly, so quickly that time itself felt blurred. In 2018, I began thinking about starting my family.
In research, there is never a "perfect" time. Experiments don't pause. Grants don't wait. Research articles don't care about your personal life. Still, I chose to move forward.
I got pregnant.

From the very beginning, I was deeply happy. I did not experience pregnancy as fear or interruption. I experienced it as joy. Carrying life brought a quiet steadiness, a gentle excitement that stayed with me even on long workdays.
Small moments surprised me with warmth. In elevators and coffee corners, colleagues would smile and ask, "How far along are you?" Each time, a quiet happiness rose inside me. Those simple questions made the pregnancy visible, shared, and real.
What made this phase even more meaningful was the environment around me. During my pregnancy, I was

surrounded by some of the world's top scientists, professors, and researchers. I often felt blessed to be carrying life while being held within a space of intellect, respect, and care. Science continued. Conversations continued. Curiosity continued. And so did life, growing quietly within me.

My pregnancy unfolded inside laboratories, between experiments, seminars, presentations, and long workdays. I was busy, but I was also supported. My colleagues treated me with respect and dignity.

Yet during my final trimester, I was diagnosed with gestational diabetes. Life became more demanding, physically and emotionally. Sleep fragmented. Twice a week, I went for ultrasound checkups. From there, I went straight to the lab. Insulin injections followed every meal. Glucose levels had to be recorded constantly.

The mental load was heavy. But what weighed on me most was the pressure to finish experiments before maternity leave, so my projects would not fall behind. I felt responsible not just for myself, but for timelines, collaborators, and expectations.

I still remember working in the lab at 10 p.m., just forty-eight hours before delivery. Before going to the hospital, I prepared a research presentation.

Looking back now, I don't know whether that intensity was right or wrong. At the time, research had narrowed my vision. I could see little beyond responsibility.

In April 2019, our daughter was born.

With her arrival, something fundamental shifted inside me. I was overwhelmed not by fear, but by love. Becoming a mother felt right, like the correct season of life.
My daughter arrived like an ocean of love, limitless, calming, complete. She still is.

Being a woman, being an elder sister, having a daughter felt like a divine blessing. In her, I saw my own childhood reflected to me. Whenever I was with her, I found myself simply looking at her, quietly, endlessly, as if she was a living painting.

She looked like a little doll, with chubby cheeks and a warm, soft body that reminded me of a small bunny curled into my arms.
She was my life then.
She is my life now.
And she always will be.
Motherhood did not take anything away from me. It expanded me.
We were first-time parents, stepping into a world we had never rehearsed for. There were no manuals, no elders in the next room, no familiar hands to guide us through those fragile early days. No one from my family could come. The distance was real, not just geographic, but emotional in the way only new motherhood can make you feel.

Those first weeks were a blur of exhaustion, uncertainty, and quiet resilience. Sleep came in fragments. Healing took patience. Every small decision felt heavy with consequence. In that unfamiliar space, friends became our support system. They cooked meals when we forgot to eat. They held the baby so I could rest. They watched over me as much as they watched over the child. Looking back, I understand it now as a divine arrangement, support arriving exactly where blood relations could not.

At the same time, I noticed something unexpected within myself. Without consciously planning to, I began repeating patterns I had once observed in my own mother during her postpartum years, how she held the baby, how she moved through fatigue, how care was offered silently before it was ever asked for. It was knowledge not learned from books or instructions, but carried through memory. In that moment, I realized how deeply wisdom travels, quietly, generationally, waiting for the day it is needed.

After three months of maternity leave, I returned to the lab, leaving my three-month-old daughter with a nanny. Every morning felt like leaving a piece of my heart behind. I cried every single day.

But options were limited. In the United States, childcare leave is brief, and the idea of "choice" often exists only on paper. Recovery timelines do not bend for policy, and newborn needs do not wait for institutional empathy. Decisions had to be made quickly, and none of them felt complete or correct.
This became the most emotionally demanding phase of my life.

When I was at home, I felt I was not working enough, falling behind, losing momentum, becoming invisible in a system that rewards uninterrupted productivity.

When I was at work, I felt I was not mothering enough, missing moments, outsourcing care, questioning my own presence.

Sleep schedules and feeding schedules merged with experiments and meetings. Alarms replaced instincts. Days were measured in pumping sessions, deadlines, and minutes of rest. I moved through routines with precision but little pause. Life felt mechanical, almost robotic, not because it lacked meaning, but because there was no space left to feel it.

The exhaustion was not only physical. It was cognitive. Emotional. The constant switching between roles left no room to be fully in either. Yet life continued. Slowly. Relentlessly. I showed up because there was no alternative, and in doing so, I learned a quiet truth: sometimes survival itself is work.

It was in the middle of this chaos that I wrote my American Heart Association postdoctoral grant.

This is a highly prestigious grant. But what that line on my CV does not show is the reality behind it. I wrote that grant while caring for a month-old baby, maintaining long lab hours, and keeping life functioning.

Doctor appointments, mine and hers.
Late-night experiments.
Feeding schedules.
Household chores.
Grant writing squeezed into exhausted hours.
Relatives visiting.

Life became a continuous juggling act. Looking back now, I often wonder how I managed it. At the time, there was no choice, only momentum. Tylenol became my closest companion.

When the grant approval letter arrived in January 2020, I stared at it in disbelief. It felt unreal, not because of recognition, but because of everything that had been carried quietly to reach that moment.
That moment was not a triumph.
It was confirmation.
Confirmation that love and labor can coexist.
That same month, my world broke open again.
In January 2020, my Nani passed away.
I had not been to India for six years. I had not seen her during that time. She had raised me. She had witnessed my childhood, my becoming. With her passing, an entire era ended, my childhood companion, my earliest witness, my emotional anchor.

The moment I received the news, I booked the next flight to India. My daughter was nine months old and did not yet have an Indian visa. I did not wait. I left her with Srikanth and traveled alone.

I could not see my Nani before she passed. That grief will always remain with me, an unfinished goodbye that never finds closure.

Later, Srikanth brought our daughter to India. For many family members, it was the first time meeting with my daughter, a meeting that carried both joy and absence.

While I was in India, news of COVID-19 emerging in China began to circulate. By the time I returned to the United States in February, cases had appeared there as well. Within weeks, the world shut down.

Life paused, carrying unresolved grief, exhaustion, and uncertainty.

I still remember the day the lockdown was announced.

Our nanny did not come that morning. At first, it felt like a small disruption, one of those minor inconveniences you expect life to absorb. By late morning, the news began to sharpen. By afternoon, everything shut down. Roads emptied. Offices closed. Phones kept buzzing with fragments of information, none of them reassuring.

I asked Srikanth to buy groceries.

What should have been a routine errand turned into an ordeal. He stood in line for nearly three hours, waiting, uncertain, surrounded by masked faces and anxious silence. When he finally returned, carrying bags heavier than they should have been, something shifted. That was the moment reality settled in.

We were alone.

No childcare. No backup. No extended family. No timeline.

Inside our home, time seemed to collapse. Outside, the world had paused. The fragile systems we relied on, help, schedules, predictability- disappeared in a single day. There was no transition period, no preparation. Just an abrupt narrowing of life to essentials: food, safety, and the small human being who depended entirely on us.

That day marked the beginning of a new kind of endurance, not dramatic, not heroic, but sustained. Quiet. Unrelenting. It was the moment we understood that survival would now happen one day at a time.
Around the same time, Srikanth received an offer letter from The Ohio State University, a milestone arriving in chaos.
With a nine-month-old baby, no childcare, and growing uncertainty, one truth became clear: we could not live apart.

To keep our family together, I resigned from my job.
I resigned from my American Heart Association grant.
It was not an impulsive decision. It came after weeks of mental accounting of energy, time, health, and what was sustainable. The environment I was leaving was not hostile. It was healthy. The science was meaningful. The work had direction. The people had become friends, colleagues who trusted me, supported me, and believed in my future.

Walking away from that was not easy.
This was not a choice between ambition and attachment. It was a choice between fragmentation and togetherness. The systems around us were already stretched thin, childcare disrupted, support networks gone, uncertainty everywhere. Holding everything together required more than efficiency; it required presence.

I chose family over career, not because my career mattered less, but because in that moment, togetherness mattered more. Science can be paused. Grants can be reapplied for. Careers, though nonlinear, can be rebuilt. But those early years of becoming a family, of supporting each other in crisis, do not return.

The decision carried loss, but also clarity. It taught me that strength is not always visible in what we accumulate. Sometimes it is expressed in what we are willing to release, so that something more fragile, and more important, can survive.
We moved to Columbus, Ohio.

And in that pause, I learned what continuity truly means, not relentless motion, but remaining whole while life rearranges itself.
In Columbus, Ohio, life slowed.
Parks replaced labs. Freight trains replaced meetings. Time returned, not as empty hours, but as spaciousness. For the first time in many years, my days were no longer ruled by clocks, deadlines, or experimental time points. They were shaped instead by sunlight, naps, seasons, and presence.
I became a full-time mother, and just as deliberately, a full-time wife.

This was not withdrawal from life. It was immersion into a different kind of work. I used this pause intentionally, raising my daughter the way I wanted to, not rushed, not outsourced, not fragmented between schedules. That quiet time gave us space to grow into parenthood together. We were learning, slowly and imperfectly, how to become a family.

I taught her how to eat, slowly, mindfully, with gratitude. Healthy food habits were not rules but rituals. Meals were unhurried. Eating became a connection, not consumption. Bubble baths became a daily joy, not a chore, warm water,

laughter, play. Walking together was not an exercise; it was a discovery. Every step was an invitation to notice.
Nature became our classroom.

We went to parks almost every day. We watched birds closely, how they perched, how they flew, how they waited. We stood quietly near ponds, watching ducks swim, geese glide, ripples forming and disappearing. In spring, we looked for bunny burrows, tiny movements in the grass that felt magical to a small child and grounding to an adult.

Our backyard turned into a sanctuary. We picnicked on the grass. We lay down and watched the sky change colors. Clouds moved slowly; so did we. I started a small kitchen garden, hands in the soil, seeds sown with hope, patience practiced daily. Growth became visible again, but on nature's timeline, not mine.

Spirituality returned to life not as philosophy, but as rhythm. We visited the temple often, not out of obligation, but out of comfort. I taught her simple shlokas, gentle mantras, small aartis, sounds meant to soothe, not instruct. Faith was introduced not as fear, but as familiarity. Bhagwan became a presence, not a pressure.

Days followed routines, predictable, slow, nourishing. Mornings unfolded gently. Evenings softened into quiet. There was repetition, yes, but also deepening. In that steadiness, both, my child and I learned to feel safe.
As much as I taught her, I was also remembering.

Much of what I passed on came from my own early years, things I had learned long before labs, grants, and conferences. I was returning to that foundational knowledge: how to be with time instead of racing it, how to observe instead of optimize, how to exist without constantly proving worth.

This pause did not make me smaller.

It made me wider.

It reminded me that growth does not always look like movement. Sometimes it looks like roots deepening quietly underground, unseen but essential.

That season gave us something precious: a bond built not in stolen minutes, but in shared days. It gave my daughter a sense of presence, and it gave me a sense of wholeness I had not known I was missing.

And when life eventually asked me to move again, I did not leave that time behind.

I carried it with me.

By the beginning of 2021, my daughter was two years old. Our days had found a rhythm. I was a full-time homemaker then, but I was not away from science. I stayed connected in quiet ways, reading scientific articles late at night, following research developments, giving the occasional invited talks, keeping my mind engaged even when my hands were busy elsewhere. Somewhere during those months, without urgency or pressure, I made a simple decision: once my child was safely vaccinated against COVID-19, I would return to work. There was no panic in that choice. No timeline announced to the world. Just clarity. The pause had done its work. I was not trying to catch up anymore. I was ready to move forward.

Reflection:

शान्तं शिवम् अद्वैतम्। , *Mandukya Upanishad 7*

True growth happens in stillness. When life quiets down, clarity shows up.

There is a version of success that rarely gets written about, the kind that unfolds quietly, without applause, while life slows down instead of speeding up. It does not come with titles or promotions. It arrives disguised as repetition, routine, care, and patience.

This chapter of my life taught me that continuity is not the same as momentum.

For years, continuity meant output, papers, experiments, grants, deadlines, progress reports, move up and up. I believed that staying relevant required constant movement. I believed that if I slowed down, I would disappear. But motherhood, grief, and a global pause showed me something different: continuity is about staying whole, not staying fast.

When I stepped into full-time motherhood, my days lost their sharp edges. There were no conference calls, no experimental time points, no urgent emails. Instead, there were meals to prepare slowly, small hands learning to hold a spoon, bubble baths filled with laughter, and walks that had no destination. At first, my mind resisted the quiet. I felt the pull of productivity, the discomfort of not "doing enough."

But slowly, I learned to listen to the rhythm of life again.

Nature does not rush. Children do not hurry their growth. Seeds do not bloom because someone demands results. They grow because conditions are right. That realization changed how I understood my own journey.

Raising my daughter during that pause did not pull me away from who I was, it returned me to myself. Teaching her how to eat mindfully, how to walk slowly, how to notice birds, ducks, clouds, and trees reminded me that learning does not only happen in classrooms or laboratories. It happens in the presence.
I saw this clearly when my days became simple. When we watched geese glide on ponds, when we waited quietly near bunny burrows, when we visited temples and repeated gentle shlokas, not as obligation, but as comfort. Faith, like science, requires patience. Both unfold best when approached with humility and attention.

This pause also revealed something deeper: that caregiving is not an interruption to intellectual life, it is a different expression of it. Teaching a child routine, safety, curiosity, and calm requires observation, consistency, and adaptability, the same skills that science demands. The lab had trained my hands; motherhood trained my heart.
And yet, the conflict was real.

There were days when I felt invisible. Days when I wondered if I was falling behind. Days when I compared myself silently to peers who were publishing, advancing, and moving forward in visible ways. But even then, something inside me remained steady. I stayed intellectually alive, reading papers during naps, giving invited talks when possible, thinking deeply even when my hands were busy with care.

That is the part we rarely talk about: how many women carry entire worlds quietly, without calling it sacrifice, without expecting recognition.

Continuity, I learned, is not linear. It bends. It pauses. It adapts. It survives by changing form.

This chapter of my life taught me that slowing down is not failure, it is often preparation. That stillness is not emptiness, it is incubation. And that some of the most important growth happens when nothing appears to be happening at all.

If you are reading this as a PhD student, a postdoc, a working mother, or an immigrant navigating multiple identities, know this: your worth does not disappear when your output changes. Seasons of care, grief, or pause are not detours, they are part of the path.

Life does not ask us to choose between becoming and belonging. It asks us to learn how to hold both.

What looks like a pause from the outside may be deep alignment on the inside.

And alignment, unlike momentum, does not fade with time.

Questions for the Reader:

- Where in your life are you being asked to slow down instead of push harder?
- What kind of growth might be happening quietly, even if it's not visible yet?

- Who are you becoming in this season, not professionally, but humanly?
- What routines, relationships, or moments are teaching you patience right now?
- If continuity didn't mean speed, what would it look like for you?

Return Stronger, Wiser

The Rise After the Pause

(Rediscovering purpose, emotional healing, and professional reinvention in a new world)

उत्तिष्ठत जाग्रत प्राप्य वरान्निबोधत ।, *Katha Upanishad 1.3.14*

Arise. Be awake. Learn by walking the path before you.

By 2021, COVID-19 vaccines became available, and for the first time in a long while, I felt ready to return to work.

I began applying for jobs, both in academia and industry, carrying with me an added complexity that shaped every conversation: visa sponsorship. I was now an applicant with a 2.5-year career gap, motherhood written into my timeline, and immigration written into every email exchange.

It became one of the hardest professional phases of my life. There were nights when exhaustion was not physical, but emotional. After putting my daughter to sleep, I would sit quietly, refreshing my inbox again and again, waiting, hoping, bracing. I often wondered how life had brought me here: from international publications, grants, and conference halls to unanswered emails and polite rejections.

Some days, confidence felt distant.
Other days, faith carried me.
I kept reminding myself that this was not regression. This was testing.
I submitted nearly two hundred applications.
Many received no response at all.
Some ended after HR calls.
Some reached hiring managers and then stalled.
Many conversations stopped the moment visa requirements entered the discussion.

Several opportunities almost worked and then quietly collapsed.
Each rejection landed differently. Some felt procedural, others deeply personal. Over time, they accumulated, not as

failure, but as fatigue. Still, I showed up the next day. And the next.

Amid all of this, I held onto one grounding truth: my basic needs were met.
There was food on the table.
Our child was healthy.
Our home was safe.
Life was not rosy, but it was still holding us.

Life, I have learned, is not meant to be a bed of roses all the time. If it were, we would never develop patience, depth, or humility. Hard phases are not punishments. They are refinement. They slow us down so we can listen more carefully to life, to ourselves, to what really matters.
At first, I limited my job search geographically to Ohio. Then I expanded it to other places including Philadelphia. After nearly a year of persistence, I finally received an offer from a pharmaceutical company, Incyte.
That moment felt like oxygen.

But another challenge remained: the visa.
Layered onto everything was the constant uncertainty of the U.S. work-visa system, an invisible weight carried by many Indian professionals. Careers are never planned in full arcs; they are constructed in short permissions. Every role, promotion, or transition is quietly shaped by eligibility, timing, and policy shifts that sit far beyond personal control. For immigrants, effort alone is never enough. You can work hard, perform well, and still remain provisional. Stability becomes conditional. Long-term thinking about career, home, or family requires contingency planning at every step.

Even moments of achievement are tempered by the knowledge that they must be continually justified on paper. Living within this framework teaches a particular discipline: patience without passivity, ambition without entitlement. You learn to hold uncertainty alongside responsibility, and to move forward even when the ground beneath you is not guaranteed.

This is the price many Indians quietly pay when they choose to build a life in America. Alongside opportunity comes uncertainty, careers planned in short permissions, stability earned provisionally, and futures shaped as much by policy as by performance. It is an invisible bill, paid not in money alone, but in patience, adaptability, and emotional resilience.

I was eligible for the O-1A visa, reserved for individuals with extraordinary ability. Securing it required demonstrating the global impact of my scientific work, fourteen recommendation letters from renowned scientists across the world, evidence of grants, high-impact publications, scientific peer review, invited talks, and international recognitions.

Receiving the O-1A visa did more than restart my career. It restored my confidence as a scientist at a time when uncertainty had begun to feel personal. Immigration systems do not read between the lines. They do not account for caregiving, for global disruption, or for years spent holding families together. They ask for clean timelines and uninterrupted output. Every pause demands explanation.

As an immigrant scientist, I felt this pressure acutely. Stepping away from a job and a grant during the pandemic meant carrying the quiet fear that these years would be interpreted as decline rather than necessity. Yet the outcome said something else. It reminded me that pauses do not erase merit, and motherhood does not dilute capability. Work continues to speak even when the scientist behind it grows quieter for a while.

This experience is not mine alone. Across the world, women in STEM navigate careers shaped by visas, caregiving, and systemic expectations of continuity. Science itself is nonlinear, yet those who practice it are often judged by linearity. Women pause, adapt, and return, carrying depth rather than speed, resilience rather than noise.

For an immigrant scientist, this moment felt like an "agnipariksha," a trial by fire. Not simply of credentials, but of belief: belief that substance would be recognized beyond interruption, that worth would not be measured only by momentum.

Philosophy frames this simply. One is not defined by motion alone. There are seasons of action and seasons of stillness. What is real is not diminished by waiting; it matures. Identity remains intact even when expression temporarily changes.

I passed, not because the path was uninterrupted, but because I had never stopped being who I was, even when the world could not immediately see it.

I joined the pharmaceutical company (Incyte) and moved back to Philadelphia with my three-year-old daughter. At that time, Srikanth was still in Ohio.

Life in Philadelphia became tightly structured.
I woke up at 5 a.m.
Cooked.
Got myself ready.
Got my daughter ready.
Dropped her off at daycare by 8 a.m.
At work: hop between the meetings, read literature, plan and execute experiments
Pick up daughter by 5:30 p.m.
Dinner. Playtime. Sleep.
Then repeat it all.

On weekends, my daughter and I often stayed with my friend Dr. Ritu Manchanda. Her home felt like my sister's house. A few close friends quietly carried me through that period.

There were none of our parents around to help us. Often, in such situations, families travel from India to support young parents. In our case, that was not possible. Harmoniously, my husband and I managed everything ourselves.
It was not easy, but it was mutual.

This phase taught me something invaluable: life is not a one-person game. A strong, understanding partnership can carry you through seasons that no crowd can. Support does not need to be loud or large. Sometimes, one steady relationship is more stabilizing than many chaotic presences.
We took turns being strong.
We took turns being tired.
Sometimes one carried more.
Sometimes the other did.
But it was always mutual.

At work, I served as the pharmacology lead for a drug developed for patients with chronic graft-versus-host disease. I worked on its mechanism of action, regulatory documentation, and medical affairs discussions. I was deeply involved in shaping how science would be understood and translated.

I felt grateful to be back at the table, contributing meaningfully, being heard.

A year later, Srikanth joined Temple University as an assistant professor, and we reunited as a family once again. Working in pharmaceuticals made one thing clear: science in pharma advances not only through discovery, but through decisions under uncertainty. I saw how data, regulation, risk, and strategy intersect long before anything reaches patients. To contribute meaningfully at that level, scientific expertise alone was not enough.

In August 2023, I enrolled in the Executive MBA program at Drexel University, to learn the language of business, not to leave science, but to strengthen its impact.

Life became demanding in a new way: full-time job work, intense coursework, homework, exams, assignments at Drexel university, family responsibilities, and daily logistics. For 16 months, not a single day was free. In the U.S., there are no shortcuts, housework, errands, childcare, everything is managed by you. Progress came not from balance, but from endurance.
What sustained me through that stretch was the presence of like-minded classmates. When the people around you share

purpose, time becomes more intentional, effort feels lighter, and even demanding days leave behind lasting memories. Community does not remove the weight of the work, but it makes carrying it possible.
In June 2025, I received my MBA degree. My first-ever foreign degree. This was also not the part of plan as many things in my life.

The two greatest cheerleaders of my adult life, Srikanth and my daughter, Srinika, attended my convocation with unfiltered enthusiasm. Their presence in the audience felt like a quiet victory of its own. I am deeply grateful to Srikanth and Srinika, whose patience and unwavering support sustained me through the most demanding 16 months. I am equally thankful to the faculty whose guidance combined rigor with understanding, making the MBA journey possible.
And even now, the realization surprises me.

Who would have thought that the girl who once studied and taught at non-elite public school would one day complete an Executive MBA from Drexel University in Philadelphia?
Not because it was an Executive MBA, but because of the distance traveled. Across cities, countries, disciplines, identities, and belief systems. The journey was not linear. It was built through pauses, reinvention, courage, and faith.
Standing there, I did not feel pride. I felt gratitude. For the girl who kept walking, even when she did not know where the road would lead.

While the MBA demanded nights and weekends, my professional life was unfolding at full speed. At work, the drug I was leading as Pharmacology Lead, successfully completed its clinical trial. Soon after, we moved toward filing the application with the U.S. Food and Drug Administration for its use in patients with graft-versus-host disease.

The months that followed were relentless. Days blurred into nights as our team drafted the Biologics License Application. We reviewed, edited, and debated again and again. Beyond data and regulatory language, we discussed how this drug would enter the world: how it would be positioned, what its logo would represent, what story it would carry. We examined every detail, CCDS, patient leaflets, and instructions for use, because each decision would eventually touch a patient's life.

This drug became my real-world classroom. Through it, I learned every step of drug development and launch, not in theory, but in consequence. Science, regulation, strategy, and responsibility converged in real time.

On the evening of August 14, 2025, the news arrived: the FDA had approved the BLA for this drug for cGVHD patients. The announcement spread quickly across media outlets. I felt a rush of joy, sharp, quiet, and deeply satisfying.

Later, our team gathered with the company's CEO for a small celebration, cake, champagne, and shared relief. In that moment, I felt profoundly grateful. Not just for success, but for the lesson it carried: leadership is built by staying present through complexity, uncertainty, honoring details, and holding both people and purpose steady until impact becomes real.

Reflection:

If you are 23 and reading this, you may be standing at the beginning of your own long road. Life may feel open, hopeful, and full of possibilities. Or it may feel confusing, slow, and uncertain. Both are valid places to be.

When I was 23, I could not have imagined the path my life would take. I did not plan pauses. I did not plan motherhood, immigration, rejection, or reinvention. I did not even plan outcomes. What I planned, consciously or not, was effort. I planned sincerity. And I kept walking.

What this chapter shows, and what life taught me slowly, is that progress does not always look like visible advancement. Sometimes it looks like long stretches of responsibility, where results are distant, and pressure is constant. Sometimes it looks like carrying competing roles at once, learning, leading, deciding, without certainty that the work will succeed. Sometimes it looks like giving your best to something whose impact you may not see for years.
These moments do not mean you are failing. They mean you are doing real work.
Life is not meant to be smooth. If everything were easy, I would never develop patience, judgment, or emotional endurance. Hard seasons shape me in ways success alone never can. They teach me how to stay accountable, how to hold complexity, and how to keep going even when recognition is delayed.

There will be phases when you give your best and still hear nothing back. When effort is invisible. When outcomes depend on systems, timing, or decisions beyond your control. During those times, it is important to remember this: lack of immediate validation is not a measure of your worth. Often, it is simply the nature of work that matters.

You may also discover that life asks you to grow in more than one direction at once. You may be learning while leading. Building while managing uncertainty. Carrying responsibility not just for yourself, but for others. Strength, then, will not look dramatic. It will look like steadiness, showing up, thinking clearly, and taking responsibility even when no one is watching.

You will also learn that no meaningful journey is completed alone. Partnership, teamwork, and shared effort matter deeply. Progress is rarely the result of one person's brilliance; it is built through collaboration, trust, and mutual endurance. The balance will never be perfect, but when it is shared, it becomes sustainable.

As you move forward, remember this: you are allowed to pause. Pauses do not erase progress. They allow perspective to deepen. But you should not disengage from yourself. Stay mentally alive. Stay attentive. Stay committed to the work in front of you.
Your career will not follow a straight line. It will bend, slow down, restart, and evolve. Skills do not disappear during pauses, they compound. Judgment sharpens. Perspective widens. You become capable of holding more than you once imagined.

Do not rush to define yourself too narrowly. Labels can shrink futures. Life is far more layered than resumes suggest. What mattered most, what carried me through uncertainty, responsibility, and delayed outcomes, was attention. Staying present. Doing the work carefully. Trusting that sustained effort, even when quiet, was shaping something meaningful.

So, if you are young and unsure, do not panic.
If you are tired, do not assume you are finished.

If you are moving slowly, do not believe you are falling behind.

Sail slowly. Sail steadily. Keep faith.
You do not need to see the whole journey today.
You only need to keep walking, with sincerity and care.
I know it from my own example, life has a way of meeting honest effort, quietly, and in its own time.

Questions for Readers:

- When life forces a pause, do you treat it as rest or as an ending?
- How have labels limited your willingness to explore new paths?
- What strengths remain with you beyond titles or roles?
- How do you stay emotionally engaged during uncertain times?
- What direction is life quietly pointing you toward right now?

Expand With Faith

Keeping the Light Alive and Building Beyond Myself

(2026 and beyond...)

न तत्र सूर्यो भाति न चन्द्रतारकं, नेमा विद्युतो भान्ति कुतोऽयमग्निः
।
तमेव भान्तमनुभाति सर्वं
तस्य भासा सर्वमिदं विभाति — *Katha Upanishad 2.2.15*

The sun does not shine by itself. Nor the moon, nor the stars, nor lightning, nor fire. There is a deeper light that shines first. Everything else glows because of it.

When I look back now, I don't think about titles or positions. I think about how ordinary my beginning was.

I was an average student. Middle-class. Conservative family. The eldest daughter. I was expected to learn how to run a home — not build a career beyond it. There was no elite schooling. No roadmap. No visible advantage.

If anything, my start was predictable.

And yet, that ordinary beginning gave me something powerful — values, discipline, respect for effort, and a quiet faith that consistency matters more than talent.

For a long time, I didn't know where I fit. Academically. Socially. Personally.

But even then, something inside me was stirring. I didn't know what to call it. I just knew I couldn't ignore it.

Along the way, friendships shaped me. I never had many friends — and that turned out to be a gift. The few I held close stretched me. They made me think bigger. Question deeper. Imagine beyond what I could see.

I didn't realize it then, but I was drawn to growth.

My mentors changed my life in ways I cannot fully explain.

At moments when I felt uncertain, someone saw something in me I hadn't yet learned to trust. That changes you. When someone reflects your potential back to you, you stand a little taller.

My mentors didn't rescue me.
They expanded me.
They refined my strength. They kept me grounded.

And I want to tell you something honestly — people around me, have never been about calculation. I have always tried to understand the person first — their values, their intentions and mindset, before anything begins. When relationships are built on sincerity, support flows naturally.

When someone opens a door for you, they are transferring trust. And that trust becomes responsibility.

If I build anything meaningful now, it is because others once built bridges for me.

Life, of course, did not move in straight lines.

I entered unfamiliar spaces again and again — new cities, new disciplines, new countries, new people. I fell. I recalibrated. I started over.

And somewhere along the way, starting over stopped feeling like failure and started feeling like skill.

Scarcity taught me clarity. Limited resources forced discipline. When money is tight, you learn to pause. You learn what matters. You learn the difference between need *vs* want.

Even when circumstances changed, that clarity stayed. It removed noise — comparison, impulse, distraction.

And what remained was freedom.

Marriage introduced me to another culture. Migration introduced uncertainty. Motherhood introduced responsibility in a foreign land.

Strength during those years wasn't dramatic. It was practical. Showing up. Managing fatigue. Staying steady when nothing felt certain.

At some point, I stopped seeing struggle as interruption.

It became rhythm.

Not something to eliminate —
but something to move through.

If there is one pattern I've noticed in my life, it is this:

Whenever I stayed — stayed with the subject, the place, the discomfort — clarity eventually came.

Sometimes it took hours.
Sometimes days.
Sometimes years.

Rarely immediately. Never without confusion.

But steadily.

It was never about speed.
It was about staying.

Working hard is not the hardest part.
Knowing what deserves your effort is.

That clarity never came when I was rushing. It came in stillness. In small moments when I stopped trying to optimize and started listening.

In a world full of noise, stillness feels impractical.

But I learned — it is preparation.

Careers rarely move in straight lines. Labels don't define futures. Titles don't guarantee meaning.

What lasts is steadiness.

The roles in my life have changed — student, scientist, immigrant, mother, founder.

The form changed.

The light did not.

And now, at this stage, what matters most to me is this:

Whatever I have earned — as a scientist, a student, a woman — has meaning only if it helps someone else see beyond their limits.

Many people feel small not because they lack ability, but because they have never been shown that other paths exist.

My path was biomedical science.

Yours will be different.

The form doesn't matter as much as the honesty with which you live it.

If your direction feels unclear right now, I want you to know something — you do not need all the answers today.

I didn't have them either.

Borrow light if you need to. From books. From conversations. From people who expand you.

Clarity rarely arrives as a dramatic revelation.

It arrives quietly — as familiarity.

And what matters most is that you keep going. With honesty. With care. Even when the next step isn't fully visible.

That has been enough for me.

Final Reflection

If this book has offered you anything,
I hope it has offered you permission —

to imagine more freely,
to move forward without a fixed map,
to pause without guilt,
to grow without apology.

You do not need to have every answer right now.

Some seasons of your life will ask only for your full presence.

And if you can give that — sincerely and wholeheartedly —
that is enough.

Because the light you are searching for was never outside you.

It has always been within you.

That is Tat Tvam Asi